MW01268517

The Conservative Hand

A Manifesto to Achieve
Conservative Political Goals

John Chambers

The Conservative Hand

A Manifesto to Achieve Conservative Political Goals

Copyright © 2010 by John Chambers

TheConservativeHand.com

Contents

● ● ● ● ●
A Manifesto to Achieve Conservative Goals

Acknowledgments

Original cover art by Kim Chambers.

I would like to thank my family for their patience, suggestions, and encouragement.

I would also like to thank everyone that participated in the 2009 Tea Party movement for inspiring me to get off the sidelines.

Preface

It has been thrilling to be part of the Tea Party movement, and see power move away from the political elite and back to the grass-roots. The sleeping giant has awakened and slowed the liberal freight train, but slowing the train isn't enough. We must reverse its direction and set it on a conservative track. To do that we need more than protests and signs; we need a strategy to achieve conservative goals. This manifesto lays out a set of rules, procedures, and a new political structure that if implemented will do just that.

- We'll look at how we got here and what hasn't worked in the past, then make a commitment to stop doing those things (if you get nothing else from this book, please take away the idea that we must stop doing the things that don't achieve our goals).

The Conservative Hand
• • • • •

- Then we'll create a new system—using some insights from economics and the free market system—that will achieve our political goals.

- Redefining ourselves and the other political players we interact with from *our* perspective will allow us to quit interacting with them based upon their definition of who they are, and start interacting with them based on our definition.

- We're going to create a new political organization. Not a primary party (like the Republican Party) or an independent third-party (like the Reform Party). It will be located in between those two entities, being part primary party and part third-party—a second-party. This party will operate unlike any existing political organization.

- We'll define a new standard for politicians: productivity. Rather than accept vague campaign promises, politicians will commit to accomplishing *our* goals.

- Borrowing some tools from the business world will enable us to create those goals and measure a politician's productivity.

- We are going to formulate incentives for politicians that reward them for achieving our goals, and punish them for failing.

- Finally, we're going to define a set of rules — something to guide us in our daily activities.

The result will be a new political framework that will allow us to achieve our political goal — enacting conservative legislation. Expect to hear frequent negative comments about this strategy (even from steadfast conservatives). After you've listened to their negative comments, listen to their solutions. Odds are they will just be rehashing the same old haven't-worked-in-the-past ideas. It's time we do something different — something that works.

Establishment Republicans and Republican politicians both jealously guard their positions and power. Sadly, many are anything but conservative. The term "Rockefeller Republican" is decades older than the term RINO (Republican in name only), but both stand for the same thing: a liberal leaning Republican. The current system — the Republican Party drifting to the left and no one closely examining their actions — works great for them. They aren't going to be any happier with us than they are with the Tea Party movement.

The Conservative Hand

• • • • •

I can't speak for anyone else, but I didn't get involved in politics for fun, as a hobby, or because I have too much time on my hands. I became involved to achieve a set of goals—goals I know will create a better country for my family, children, and grandchildren. I'm sacrificing part of my life to achieve those goals. I don't need good intentions or a strong effort from politicians, I need results. A politician that tries hard and fails needs to be replaced with a politician that tries hard and succeeds.

It's time to unleash our conservative hand, leave our fingerprints on the political system, and put our country back on the right track.

John Chambers

Introduction

I sit here after the Republican catastrophe of 2008 and wonder what went wrong. The Republican Party has gone through many changes since I became interested in politics in the late '60s. The Republican and the Democratic parties were not that far apart at the time. While most would have pointed to economics as the biggest difference between the parties, Richard Nixon famously said "We are all Keynesians now." How different could the parties have been if both were followers of economist John Maynard Keynes' big government economic theories?

The Democratic Party started moving left in 1968. Their leftward shift has been relentless. Today ideas such as the redistribution of wealth, nationalization of health care, and removal of all abortion restrictions are not only accepted, but considered establishment Democratic thought. While conservatives are appalled at what has happened to the Democratic Party, the base of the Democratic Party believes in these ideas. For better or worse, the Democratic Party represents its members' ideology.

The same cannot be said of today's Republican Party.

A major shift in Republican thought took place with the 1980 election of Ronald Reagan, who had different ideas about economics, foreign policy, defense, and social issues. It was dubbed Reaganism. For the first time in a generation, the Republican Party became the driving force in shaping government policy. After four years of what the press called "radical, right-wing, conservative government" Reagan was reelected in 1984, winning 49 of 50 states (and coming within a few thousand votes of winning all 50 states). It was the most lopsided presidential victory in American history.

In 1988 George H. W. Bush ran on a platform of continuing Reagan's policies. Bush tied himself so closely to Reagan that many called the 1988 election Reagan's third election. Bush won in a landslide, winning 40 states including Democratic strongholds California and New Jersey.

After the election it became apparent that the man who had once called Reagan's economic proposals "voodoo economics" was no Reaganite. Bush advocated a "kinder and gentler" conservatism (with its implied message that conservatism was somehow unkind and ungentle), and governed from the center rather than from the right as Reagan had. The result was a 1992 loss to Democrat Bill Clinton. Bush only managed to carry 18 states, less than half the amount he carried in 1988 running as a Reagan conservative.

In 1994, a band of rogue Republicans in the House of Representatives proposed *The Contract with America*—ten legislative proposals rooted in conservatism. Their leader, Newt Gingrich, was roundly criticized by the press as being a radical conservative (*Newsweek's* cover headlined "How the Gingrinch Stole Christmas"). The result was a major Republican victory. For the first time in 40 years, the Republicans took control of both houses of congress.

Everything was set for a Republican presidential win in 1996. Conservatism was on the rise while President Clinton's liberal policies had been unpopular. The Republicans nominated...Sen. Bob Dole. He had been one of the "cooler heads" in the senate that had blocked the enactment of many of *The Contract With America's* propositions. Bob Dole was a moderate and proud of it. He badly lost an election Republicans should have won. Strangely, many Republican insiders seemed happier losing with a moderate Republican than winning with a conservative.

George W. Bush ran in 2000 as a "compassionate conservative" (another Republican running on an implied message that there is something wrong with plain-old conservatism). Despite reassurances from people like Karl Rove that Bush "really got

Reagan and conservatism," few Reagan supporters would recognize the economic and domestic policies Bush implemented. Watching the series of bailouts implemented by the Bush administration, I heard Nixon's words echoing in my head—"We are all Keynesians now."

When Bush accepted the Republican nomination in 2000 the Republicans held majorities in both the Senate and House of Representatives. By the time Bush left office the Democrats held a filibuster-proof majority in the senate (60 Democrat vs. 40 Republican) and an enormous majority in the House (257 Democrat vs. 178 Republican).

In 2008 the Republicans nominated John McCain. The most far left Republican candidate since, well ever! There were rumors in 2004 that the Democratic nominee (John Kerry) was going to ask McCain to be the VP candidate on the Democratic ticket. Imagine if anyone had floated that idea about Newt Gingrich or Ronald Reagan! Who knows if the McCain VP rumor was true, but the fact that it was taken seriously shows how far to the left McCain had been in the past.

McCain lost to the most radically left presidential candidate in history (carrying only 22 states). Other than McCain's spirited defense of the war in Iraq, it was difficult to pinpoint the differences between McCain and Obama on any major issue.

The Conservative Hand

● ● ● ● ●

We're already hearing calls that the Republican Party needs to move left. This is a recurring theme after every election, regardless of outcome. We expect Democrats to shift left (that's what they are—a leftist party), but the Republican Party's continual move to the left leaves conservatives without a party truly representing their views or trying to achieve conservative goals.

A Review of What Doesn't Work

Insanity is doing the same thing over and over again expecting different results. Despite what the typical liberal would tell you, conservatives are not insane. Still, when asked what conservatives should do to take back the country from its current liberal domination you often hear conservatives recycling the same old ideas that haven't worked in the past. Let's take a look at some of the things that haven't worked, and then quit acting as though we're insane.

A Conservative Messiah

In Reagan we had the closest thing to a conservative messiah we'll ever get, and we weren't able to permanently transform the Republican establishment or American society. Sadly, as soon as Reagan left office the Republican Party reverted to its previous form, and America once again started to drift left.

The Conservative Hand
● ●●●●

The left follows Saul Alinsky's *Rules for Radicals*. Rule 12 is "Pick the target, freeze it, personalize it, and polarize it." In other words, make a movement about a man, then attack the man. One of the great strengths about the Tea Party movement has been its lack of a central figure for the left to attack. I remember several times this spring seeing Democratic operatives (1) express frustration over not having an individual in the Tea Party movement to attack, and (2) attempt to make the Tea Party movement about a single person so they could attack that person.

Failing in their attempt to make the Tea Party movement about a single person, they attacked the group as a whole. What did their attack accomplish? Nothing, the left's attempts to attack the Tea Party movement—portraying its members as astroturf, racists, selfish, rich, uneducated, and even too well dressed—failed miserably.

It's notable that the only people who want to make the Tea Party movement about an individual are those on the right that have already formed a cult-like following around an individual, and those on the left that want to personalize the movement so they can attack it. Neither have the best interest of the Tea Party movement at heart.

Movements that survive and grow over time are not about men, they are about ideas. Conservatism has survived because it is about the ideas and truths stated in *The Declaration of Independence* and *The United States Constitution*: individual freedom and limited government; rights granted not by the government, but endowed by our maker. Creating a conservative messiah is a losing strategy for conservatism.

Third-Parties

Our "winner takes all" political system forces us into a two-major-party setup. The last time a major-party failed and was replaced by another was in the 1850's (and it took the Civil War to actually end the Whig Party). Supplanting either of the major political parties would be a daunting—as in not going to happen in our lifetime—task.

What happens when a *serious* third-party does arise? In 1912, Teddy Roosevelt became upset with the Republican Party and formed a third-party: the Bull Moose Party. The result was a Democratic victory (Bull Moose 27%, Republican 23%, Democrat 42%). In 1992 people were so dissatisfied with George H. W. Bush's lack of conservative principles it opened the door for Ross Perot to form the Reform Party. The result was another Democratic victory (Reform 19%, Republican 37%, Democrat 43%). Note the Democratic vote amount in both cases was in the low 40% range. The only thing these third-parties accomplished was to allow Democrats to win without getting a majority of the vote.

If we establish another serious third-party will the Republican Party move to the right in an effort to get those conservative voters back? They never have in the past, why would anyone think they would in the future? Establishment Republicans believe the effort to get anyone to cross party lines (whether Democrat or third-party) is too high to be worth the cost. It is easier to shift to the left and go after the non-committed moderate/swing voter. Yes Virginia, the practical effect of conservative third-parties has been to shift the Republican Party to the *left*. To them it's just a marketing problem. If conservative third-parties are eating away at your right, you need to shift left to pick up more votes.

How many political third-parties can you name? At the moment there are at least 85; eighty-damn-five! How much political impact do these 85 third-parties have? None; nada; zero! Conservatives have put a lot of time and effort into third-parties and they have accomplished nothing. We need to abandon strategies like third-parties that don't achieve conservative goals and refocus on strategies that will achieve our goals.

Political Action Committees

Special interest groups routinely form political action committees (PACs) to get their message out and influence elections. They are used heavily by groups from all parts of the political spectrum. Conservatives have invested heavily in PACs, and we've had good results from using them in the past, but only *good* results.

If PACs were the answer to our problem, the problem would have been eliminated long ago. Not only are conservative goals not being met, but we're actually moving backwards. Political action committees have their place, but are not the solution to achieve conservative goals.

The Republican Party

Conservatives assumed that if they worked to elect Republicans it would help to achieve conservative goals. History has shown that assumption to be false. What have we gotten in return for our loyalty? A Republican Party dominated by big-government RINOs primarily concerned about maintaining their personal power.

What is the real goal of the Republican Party? To quote one local Republican Party website: "The Republican Party's purpose is to search and find Republican candidates for all partisan and local non-partisan offices. Its role is to also support the Republican candidates who volunteer to run for an elected office." In other words, elect Republicans (any Republican—tall, short, skinny, fat, conservative, liberal, honest, or dishonest; as long as they call themselves "Republican" the party's goal is to elect them).

Conservatives must come to grips with a basic fact: the Republican Party does not share our goals and simply electing Republicans is not sufficient to achieve conservative goals.

The Conservative Hand

● ● ● ● ●

Controlling the Republican Party from the Inside

It's tempting to think we can take over the Republican Party by placing conservatives in key positions so they can influence the party's direction. Unfortunately, that strategy is dependent on people and personalities. Many of today's party insiders that are trying to move the party to the left joined the Republican Party during the Reagan era as solid conservatives. So what happened? Some have succumbed to the political equivalent of the Stockholm syndrome. Eventually conservative Republican insiders come to identify themselves as Republicans rather than conservatives. Their loyalty and self-interest shifts to the Republican Party. At that point they become establishment Republicans and part of the problem.

We also have to ask the obvious question: so what if we take control of the Republican Party from the inside? Have the bureaucrats in the Republican Party ever been able to control their office holders? Do Republican politicians take their marching orders from the head of the Republican Party? Would conservatives controlling from the inside have any more influence than current party members? No, no, and double no. Controlling the Republican Party from the inside will not achieve conservative goals.

A New Approach

Now that we've established what doesn't work, let's try a new approach. Ironically, because our system forces us into a two-major-party setup the Republican Party is the only *practical* political tool to achieve our goals, but we need to interact with it in a new way. We must establish a new relationship with the Republican Party, and a new system that allows us to control the party and politicians instead of allowing them to control us.

Economist Adam Smith's described the phenomenon of people pursuing their economic self-interest resulting in the common good as the free market's invisible hand. It seems counter intuitive to think that a diverse set of individuals pursuing their individual goals (in other words: chaos) can achieve a broader common goal. Yet, that is exactly what happens.

There is also an invisible hand that drives politics. People take up a political cause for any number of reasons (logical, emotional, altruistic, selfish, etc...); their motivation isn't important. What is important is that once a person becomes attached to a goal it becomes their political self-interest, and moving it forward is the coinage they seek. At the end of the day, despite the often soaring rhetoric, everyone works in their political self-interest.

Knowing this concept from economics also applies to politics, let's use it to create a new political system to achieve our goals.

A New Definition of the Players

The first step in creating our system is to redefine all the players we've been interacting with from *our* perspective.

Defining Conservatives

The political goal of conservatives is to enact conservative legislation. The groups we form, candidates we support, and actions we take must all move that goal forward. Everything we do must be measured against that goal. A political conservative is someone who seeks to enact conservative legislation.

Defining the Republican Party

What is the Republican Party? From our standpoint, it is a tool for achieving conservative goals—and nothing more.

Does it sound like I want to take advantage of the Republican Party? Go back to the mid-1800's and you'll run into a group of people forming a new political party for the purpose of "abolishing slavery and restricting the role of government in economic and social life." Notice anything? The Republican Party was formed as a tool to achieve specific goals.

- The goal of the Republican Party's founders: abolish slavery and restrict the role of government in economic and social life.
- The goal of today's establishment Republicans: elect Republicans.

An institution that was established to end the abomination of slavery has been reduced to little more than a sports team. Winning for winning's sake has become the Republican Party's goal.

No doubt establishment Republicans will accuse us of many things, from disloyalty to not being team players. Look at what they want us to do—abandon our self-interest for the "good of the party." What's the point of simply electing Republicans without a purpose? It's like starting a trip without a destination. Is it any wonder that in 2008 the party was described as directionless? We should "support" the Republican Party in ways designed to achieve our goals, not theirs.

The goal of the Republican Party is to elect Republicans. Our goal is to enact conservative legislation; from our standpoint the Republican Party is a tool we use to enact conservative legislation—and nothing more.

Defining Politicians

Why do we elect politicians to office? We elect them to achieve conservative goals. So what is a Republican politician? They are the same as the party, a tool for achieving conservative goals.

Office holders disagree—especially those that have comfortably held office for a while. They say "Our experience has made us wise; trust us; look to us for leadership." Elected office more often produces hubris than wisdom. Take the 2008 bank bailout bill. It's obvious the Republican members of the House and Senate didn't understand the problem, didn't understand the bill (most didn't even read it), and voted for it out of fear because they were told by an unelected bureaucrat the economy would crash without it. Voting yes on a bill out of fear and ignorance is not a sign of wisdom or leadership.

The goal of politicians is to get elected. Our goal is to enact conservative legislation; from our standpoint a Republican politician is a tool we use to enact conservative legislation—and nothing more.

A New Organization—The Second-Party

We've seen that becoming loyal Republican Party members doesn't achieve our goals, and neither do third-parties. What we need is something in between the primary Republican Party and third-parties; an organization that stands alone like a third-party, but that also controls the primary Republican Party—a secondary (or second) party.

Second-parties *are* partisan political parties. They will endorse and support candidates and have members just like any other political party. All of the normal activities of the major political parties are within the scope of a second-party: raising money, running advertisements, holding rallies, and printing support materials.

They are not a subset of the Republican Party. Second-parties are 100% independent parties; they will not take money, guidance, or even chewing-gum from the Republican Party. The Republican Party is already discussing how they can bring the Tea Party movement *into* the Republican Party. Their goal is to co-opt, control, and use the Tea Party movement to achieve Republican Party goals. It will attempt to do the same with any second-party that cozies up to it. We are going to use the Republican Party as a tool to achieve *our* goals; we are not going to be their tools.

Second-parties will not field candidates, rather they will endorse only Republican politicians. Focusing our efforts this way will make us a valuable ally (and terror) to the Republican Party. The Democrats have organizations like unions and community organizing groups that provide invaluable support to Democrats while constantly pushing the Democratic Party to the left. The Republican Party has no equivalent organizations pushing it to the right (one of the reasons it continually drifts left). Second-parties can perform that function.

Besides endorsing candidates, second-parties will *reject* candidates. Rejecting a Republican politician means none of the second-party's members will support that politician in any way: votes, money, yard signs, working in their campaign, nothing. Moreover, it means the second-party's members will work against the rejected politician to prevent their election.

Will second-parties support Democrats or third-parties? Never! They will *reject* all Democratic and third-party candidates. A second-party that supports either a Democratic or third-party candidate is by definition not a second-party.

The Conservative Hand
● ● ● ● ●

They have broken the system and turned themselves into just another special interest group, which is something we know doesn't work to achieve conservative goals.

Second-parties are built around the accomplishment of a single goal. This goal can be broad (returning the federal government to its constitutional bounds) or narrow (the repeal of one bill), but it must be a single, clearly defined goal. There is a solid reason for single-goal second-parties. Second-parties are the political equivalent of small businesses. Quicker on their feet and more creative than the corporate giants—small businesses are the engine of innovation in our economy. Second-parties are designed to be the engine of innovation in politics.

A second-party with multiple goals is the political version of a corporate conglomerate. Very little original thought comes out of conglomerates. They usually "innovate" by buying out a smaller company that has come up with a good idea. Turn on a dime? The phrase "trying to make an elephant dance" was coined to describe the agility of the typical conglomerate.

The rule is: two goals, two parties, one goal per party. This means both goals will be worked on simultaneously and always receive the attention they deserve. Does this mean you have to be a single issue voter? No. What it does mean though, is that if you want to achieve multiple goals you should join (or form) multiple second-parties.

The Conservative Hand
• • • • •

Does this mean second-parties must act as though they exist in a vacuum? Do businesses act as though they operate in a vacuum? No, they coordinate activities with other businesses, but they always do so with their own self-interest in mind. Second-parties should take the same approach with other second-parties.

Second-parties will not have a platform. A political platform is a series of political statements that is ignored before the ink is dry—its purpose is to placate the party's core, not guide politicians. Besides, platforms are made up of multiple (often conflicting) goals. This violates our one goal rule. Second-parties will have a statement-of-purpose and a goal-set.

A statement-of-purpose is a one page document that describes why the second-party was formed and what it intends to accomplish. *The Declaration of Independence* contains all of our country's founding concepts, and it is only one page long. If you can't describe your purpose in a single page, then your purpose is too vague.

A goal-set is a series of goals that build upon each other to achieve a larger goal. In plain language, a long-term plan for achieving a goal. You may only have one goal, but you need a plan to get there. No goal is too large to accomplish if you break it down into small enough steps. That's all a goal-set is: a large goal that has been broken down into a series of smaller goals that are steps to accomplishing the larger goal.

The Conservative Hand

• • • • •

The statement-of-purpose and goal-set are published documents. We must be open about what we want to accomplish, and how we intend to get there. (1) This will allow the party's members to evaluate the second-party and determine if they want to support it. (2) We don't want to go down the dark road of Saul Alinsky's hidden agendas and duplicitous schemes that progressives long ago embraced. Now that some daylight is being shined on their methods we are starting to see these techniques backfire—big time.

Unlike unions and other progressive organizations that use a top-down socialist model (which always results in the leadership being out of sync with the members), we're going to use a free-market model. In a real sense the members are the customers of any second-party. Second-parties will have to compete with each other for members. Total transparency allows members to evaluate a second-party and determine if its goal is worthwhile, if its plan for achieving that goal makes sense, if it is supporting truly productive politicians, and if the party is achieving its goals. Just like a company that produces an inferior product loses its customers and goes under, second-parties that aren't achieving their goals will lose members and go under—to be replaced by another second-party that will achieve those goals.

Second-parties set productivity goals for politicians, and measure politicians on whether they achieved or failed to achieve those goals. Both the goal setting process and measurement process are different from what has been used in politics in the past. Endorsement or rejection of a politician will be based solely on the politician's productivity measurement.

Second-parties can be any size—from two members to thousands. They can be as local as the county commissioner's race, or as national as a presidential race.

Adam Smith's invisible hand causes many individual businesses pursuing their self-interest to achieve a greater good: an efficient free market system. Second-parties, each pursuing their self-interest, will form our invisible conservative hand and achieve a greater good: moving the country back to the principles it was founded upon.

A New Standard—Productivity

What's a promise made without the intent of keeping it? Manipulation. A promise means nothing. Productivity is the only thing that matters, and it must be measured in real accomplishments: *measurable* actions that move an issue towards legislative enactment.

What's Not Productivity

Giving politicians credit for doing the same things that haven't worked in the past is another form of insanity. Politicians have developed many ways to make it look like they are advancing an issue that are really designed to give them political cover. The following list isn't complete, but it gives us an idea of the kind of activities to look out for.

The Conservative Hand
● ● ● ● ●

Letter Writing

An infamous example from the 2008 presidential campaign was Sen. Obama's 2006 "warning" letter to the Secretary of the Treasury about Freddie and Fannie. He constantly brought it up during the campaign to show he was ahead of the curve on the economic meltdown. If you read the actual letter, it boils down to "I have no idea if there is a problem or even what kind of problem might someday occur, but just on the outside chance some kind of problem comes up in the future I'm writing you this letter to cover my ass."

How much attention do you pay to the junk mail you get in your mail box? These letters are the political equivalent of junk mail. They are opened by some staff member and filed away to never be seen again. The only purpose of writing these things is to give a politician cover on an issue and make it look like they are doing something productive.

Co-Signing Bills

It's easy for a Republican to attach their name to a bill as a co-signer, but does that mean they are working to actively advance the issue? The vast majority of Republicans in the house co-signed the 2007 Fair Tax bill. I have seen hour upon hour of interviews with Republican house members discussing taxes. How many times during those tax discussions did they inject the Fair Tax? The passing mentions could be counted on your fingers. The times they vigorously advocated the Fair Tax can be counted by touching the tips of your thumb and first finger. They co-signed the bill then promptly forgot about it. That's not support, much less productivity.

Preaching to the Choir

The fair tax is an issue that "will never pass" according to pundits. Thirty years ago universal health care was a "will never pass" issue. Yet, here we sit with an expectation that it will become a reality sometime during Obama's presidency. What's the difference? In any discussion of health care, Democrats will inject the point that "the solution to this problem is a universal health care system." They have enthusiastically and without apology promoted their position, and not just in front of partisan, liberal audiences, but in front of every audience.

How does Republicans' productivity on the Fair Tax bill compare? Rarely mentioning it outside of the friendly confines of a Fair Tax rally or newsletter, their work has amounted to little more than "preaching to the choir" (and just enough preaching to secure the choir's vote). That's not productivity, that's pandering.

Letter writing, co-signing, and preaching to the choir are three examples of faux productivity. We must quit giving politicians credit for activities that don't achieve conservative goals.

Defining Productivity Goals

If something can't be measured, it doesn't exist. We need to set measurable goals, and require Republicans to accomplish those measurable goals.

Anyone that has worked in the corporate world for any amount of time is familiar with SMART goals. They were developed to focus employees on specific activities and eliminate the wiggle room many employees abuse so they seem more productive than they actually are. Instead of passively allowing politicians to make promises to us, we'll set goals for politicians and bluntly ask them to commit to accomplishing those goals. We elect politicians to achieve our conservative goals, not their own.

What is a SMART goal?

> **S** Specific. Not "I support lower taxes", but "I will cut income taxes 10% by June of this year."

> **M** Measurable. You need some way to define if the action was completed, and it must be in the form of a yes or no question. "Were income taxes cut 10% by June of this year?" If you can't phrase the goal as a yes or no question then you should restate the goal or break it down into a series of more specific sub-goals.

> **A** Action Oriented. "*I support* lower taxes" requires no action on the part of the politician. "*I will* cut income taxes by 10% by June of this year" does require action.

R Realistic. "I will cut income taxes *50%* by June of this year" is not a realistic promise. Politicians make unrealistic promises, because they know they will never be held to them.

T Time bound. Establishing a deadline allows us to hold politicians' feet to the fire for not achieving conservative goals (and properly reward them for achieving conservative goals). "I will cut income taxes 10% *by June of this year.*"

Large goals should be broken down into a series of smaller goals: a *goal-set*. Your goal-set will become the plan for achieving your larger goal. If you ever determine a goal is too large to achieve, break it down into a series of smaller goals. There is no goal too large to achieve if you break it down into small enough sub-goals.

A New Measurement

We need to establish a standard to determine if a politician is achieving conservative goals. Before we do that, let's look at what hasn't worked in the past.

What Hasn't Worked—Ratings

The American Conservative Union defines anyone with an 80+ rating as a "standout ACU conservative." That would include Lindsey Graham (89% lifetime rating) who supports amnesty for illegal aliens, Cap and Trade, voted for the TARP bank bailout, and in many people's minds is the poster child for the term RINO. How does someone like that end up with a standout conservative rating?

Composite ratings allow politicians to game the system. As long as they reach some magic number they can brag they are conservatives, but are they? Do they really focus on conservative issues, or do just enough to get by? What about that 10%-20% of issues they aren't conservative on. Did they give lukewarm support to those liberal issues, or did they work tirelessly for them (as John McCain, who also holds a solid conservative grade from the ACU, has done).

The current system for rating politicians is all but useless. They haven't worked in the past to make politicians more conservative, why would we think they would work in the future. Do you remember the definition of insanity?

Productive vs. Non-Productive

We need a simple pass/fail standard that gives politicians nowhere to hide. They are either productive (because they achieved conservative goals) or non-productive (because they failed to achieve conservative goals).

We're setting the agenda for politicians; demanding they accomplish our goals. If we let politicians off the hook by rewarding them for "trying hard but failing," then that's all we'll ever get. Failure is failure. Politicians that try hard but fail need to be replaced with politicians that try hard and succeed.

We must deal with politicians that make promises with no intention of keeping them. Setting SMART goals and using a pass/fail grade will pin these charlatans down. They'll have to think twice before agreeing to the goal in the first place (knowing they will have to accomplish it) and we'll have an objective measurement to determine if they support our goals or were just paying them lip-service to gain our support.

Finally, a pass/fail measurement will discipline us in creating our goals. It won't be enough to just state some large goal; we'll have to think about *how* to get from here to there. We'll be forced to break our large goal down into a series of smaller, realistic goals that lead to the accomplishment of our larger goal. Do you know what they call a series of smaller goals that lead to the accomplishment of a larger goal? A plan, something that has been missing from the conservative lexicon for far too long.

Productive (accomplished the goal) and non-productive (failed to accomplish the goal) are the only two acceptable measurements. If neither describes the politician's work, then the goal was incorrectly set. Change the goal, not the measurement system.

A New Action Plan

Now that we have this new system, how do we use it to get politicians to accomplish our goals? We're going to use an old variation on the "carrot and stick" approach. Politicians can accept our positive incentives (the carrot) or we'll nudge them on with some negative incentives (we'll beat them with the stick). The key though, is that the positive incentive is always available to them should they choose to accept it.

Positive Incentives—The Carrot

As a true political party, we can give a candidate everything a regular political party can give them: money, campaign workers, advertising, commercials, signage, and we'll bring one more thing the Republican Party can't—*votes*. Because our second-party members are committed to voting for the candidate our second-party endorses, it guarantees the candidate a specific number of votes. That's the reason it is important to vote in every election—primary, regular, run-off, and special. We must become reliable voters; voters politicians can bank their careers on.

We also have to be reliable in more ways than voting. Democrats have entities like unions and community-organizing groups that provide reliable grass-roots support. The Republican Party doesn't have any equivalent entities. Second-parties can fill that void; actively and reliably supporting productive Republican candidates. This is a large carrot (incentive) for any Republican politician.

A second-party should only endorse one candidate in any race, even if there are multiple productive politicians running in a primary. Endorsing multiple candidates splits your vote and waters down your influence. Conservatives splitting their vote in the primaries enabled John McCain to secure the 2008 Republican presidential nomination. Focusing on multiple candidates decreases our influence; focusing on a single candidate amplifies our influence.

Remember we said second-parties are the political version of small businesses—the engine of innovation in the business world? This is where it pays off. We're going to be the engine of political ideas; coming up with new and innovative ways to support candidates.

Negative Incentives—The Stick

We're going to create several new methods to chasten non-productive politicians. We'll also be eliminating some long-standing practices used to punish politicians that have historically had a negative effect on achieving our goals.

The most common ways for conservative voters to show their dissatisfaction with a Republican candidate is to either not vote at all or vote for the Democratic candidate to punish the Republican. Both must stop now, because both actions push the Republican Party to the *left*. When conservatives fail to vote, establishment Republicans consider them to be unreliable voters. Since their conservative voters are unreliable, they move to the left to pick up more voters. And what do you think establishment Republicans think when you vote Democratic to punish a Republican candidate? In their minds, anyone that would even consider voting Democratic is by definition a moderate/swing voter, and the way to pick up those voters is to move to the left.

Stop performing actions that push the Republican Party to the left. We're going with a new strategy: creating political holes.

Political Holes

How do you vote in every election when the only options are a rejected Republican candidate, a Democratic candidate, and a third-party candidate? You write someone in, but not just anyone. If a second-party has rejected the Republican candidate, they need to establish a write in candidate for that office. It can be any name (personally, I like A. Conservative), but it needs to be clearly related back to a specific second-party. When the votes are tallied, it will be clear to the rejected candidate and Republican Party how many votes they could have had, if they had been productive. Those missing votes are *voter holes*.

We're also going to create *support holes*. A support hole is the withdrawing of any type of support whatsoever. No money, yard signs, grass-roots support, nothing. This is harder to gauge, but this type of behind the scenes support is the life-blood of most political campaigns. When it goes away they feel it.

Rejection Notices

A rejection notice is when we actively work against a non-productive politician to either prevent their election or remove them from office. Note this does *not* involve giving any support to Democrats or a third-party (both activities drive the Republicans to the left).

A dull knife not only does a poor job, it's dangerous because its performance is unpredictable. Non-productive politicians are the dull knives of politics. They not only do a poor job, they are dangerous because their performance is unpredictable. For physical safety, dull knives must be made sharp or replaced. For the safety of our country, non-productive politicians must be made productive or replaced.

The Conservative Hand

● ● ● ● ●

Reject and remove from office all non-productive politicians.

Be just as creative rejecting candidates as endorsing them: handbills, posters, yard signs, advertisements, word of mouth, and public protests are just a start. For example, use pink (as in pink slip) as a base color for rejection notice literature and media. Display rejected politician's signs and bumper stickers upside down (an upside down flag indicates a problem; an upside down political sign indicates a problem with the candidate).

Tea Party activists learned quickly that Republican politicians are sensitive to conservatives protesting against them. It also sends up a huge red flag in the general public's mind—if conservatives are protesting a Republican candidate there must be something wrong with him. Rejecting a candidate is just as powerful a tool as supporting a candidate.

The Rulebook

1. Our goal is to enact conservative legislation.

People choose to support politicians for a number of reasons:

- Party membership (Republican).

- Endorsements (endorsed by the local police union).

- Personality or charisma.

- Debate performance.

- A slogan (Yes America Can!—Bush 2004, Yes We Can! —Obama 2008).

- The politician is from a state or region.

- They belong to a specific religion (Catholics for Kennedy—1960).

- Endorsements by another politician or celebrity.

Special-interest groups and lobbyists don't throw their support behind a candidate for any of the above reasons; they expect the candidate to enact specific legislation in return for their support. If a candidate gets conservative support because they belong to a specific party, and they get a lobbyist's support for promises to vote a certain way on legislation, when it comes time to vote on bills how do you think they will vote? History has shown they will vote the lobbyist's line. Lobbyists understand it isn't important who is elected. What is important is that the person they support enacts their legislation.

Our goal is to enact conservative legislation. If a politician doesn't contribute to the achievement of our goal, they should be rejected and removed from office.

2. Process! Process! Process!

There is a fundamental rule for improving the quality of a product. You don't focus on the product; you focus on the processes that produced the product. If you improve the process, the end product will improve.

The product we're trying to produce isn't politicians, it is legislation. Politicians are part of the process that enacts conservative legislation. We should constantly be striving to improve our processes using a tool like the PDMRI cycle.

PDMRI stands for plan, do it, measure, review, and improve the process. It is a quality assurance tool used to improve processes and help you more efficiently and effectively achieve your goals.

- **P** Plan. Your plan includes any processes you are going to implement to achieve your goal.

- **D** Do it. Implement your plan.

- **M** Measure. Did your plan achieve your goal? This is why we spent so much time talking about having specific measurements. If you can't measure something, you can't determine its quality.

- **R** Review. Where, how, and why did your plan succeed or fail?

- **I** Improve the process. Notice this isn't just "improve," it is "improve the process." It's a mistake to focus on the end product. The quality of the end product is determined by the quality of the process that produced it.

PDMRI is a cycle. When you're done with the improve-the-process step, you circle right back to the plan step. The cycle continues over, and over, and over again. Each cycle improves your process; eliminating actions and ideas that don't work, and implementing new actions and ideas. By doing this over and over again you'll increase the effectiveness of the processes you use to implement your goals.

What PDMRI is not is a finger-pointing session. The assumption you work with is that on average, the people in

your process are average. If there is an error (Kathy forgot...,
Bob didn't..., Ted incorrectly...) it is because there is a problem
with the process. Improve the process so it will prevent these
errors in the future. As a general rule, no finger-pointing or
blame is allowed during a PDMRI session.

Drop strategies that don't work, improve working strategies,
and add new strategies.

3. Our actions must be measured against our goal.

We all know somebody that is always in motion; always busy.
Yet, when you step back and look at what they actually
accomplish the list seems kind of short for that much work.
I'm sure you can also name someone who makes you think
"how can anyone accomplish so much in so little time?" The
difference is one person stays focused on their goal—what
they want to accomplish—and the other doesn't stay focused.

Farmers have a goal of harvesting a crop at the end of the
season. Take one that works sunrise to sunset, but allows
himself to get off-track working on things that don't contribute
to his goal of harvesting a crop. What's the result at the end of
the season? His barn will be empty, because he didn't have a
crop to harvest. He worked hard. He probably even felt good
about all the hard work he was doing, but when he was
staring at an empty barn what did all that hard work count
for? Nothing.

If you don't accomplish your goal, then all the hard work you put in counts for nothing; zero; nada; zip. Determine up front if an activity is contributing to your goal. If it isn't, don't do it. Instead, spend the time on something that does contribute to achieving your goal.

4. If something doesn't work, stop doing it.

Not only conservatives, but everyone seems to have a propensity for trying the same solutions repeatedly, even if they didn't work in the past. "This time will be different" is usually the rationale, but it never is different. Strategies that always fail will always fail. Nonetheless, you will find seemingly reasonable people advocating we continue doing the same things that haven't worked in the past.

People get comfortable with a strategy; staying in a rut not because they are stuck, but because they are afraid to get out of the rut. Maybe the strategy hasn't produced the results they wanted, but they know what it involves. Changing to something new can be scary.

Some people have a one track mind. Like a pit bull, when they latch on an idea they won't let go of it. These are often the people who say "It will work this time" then advocate doing exactly the same thing in exactly the same way that hasn't worked in the past.

Others lack imagination. Everyone is gifted with different skills, and no one has all of them. Imagination is a skill some people are gifted with, and others aren't. When you can't think of anything new, the tendency is to fall back on the same old solutions (even if they don't work) and to rationalize to yourself "Well, at least we're doing something," not realizing that doing something that doesn't work is worse than doing nothing—much worse.

People become over committed to an idea or activity. When you have invested a lot into an idea, it's hard to just let it go— you feel you must see it through to the end. The business term for this is the "sunk cost effect." Countless businesses have gone bankrupt because of it. You are better off losing your sunk costs and pursing a strategy that will be profitable, instead of following your sunk cost into bankruptcy (political bankruptcy in our case).

Remember, not only is our goal is to enact conservative legislation, but all our actions must be measured against that goal. Sometimes that means getting out of your comfort zone, swallowing your pride, and letting go of ideas you have invested heavily in. If an activity isn't helping us achieve our goal, stop doing it.

That's not just a rule, that's a commandment.

5. Don't stand still.

The left chants the word change as a mantra, and by the word change they mean replace. No doubt when you replace something you do fix some problems, but what you replace it with always brings its own set of problems. This is why the left's solutions over the years have only created another new set of problems (frequently worse than the original). The correct logic for solving problems isn't *replacement-change*, it is *improvement-change*.

Ideas get stale and lose some effectiveness. That doesn't mean you should abandon those strategies, rather improve them. *7 Up* introduced "the Uncola" slogan in the 1970s. It catapulted the brand to the upper tier of soft-drink sales. They later replaced the slogan because they felt it was becoming a little stale and it was time for a change. *7 Up's* market share dropped and never recovered. Instead of abandoning the uncola strategy, they should have worked to improve it.

This doesn't mean you shouldn't think of new ideas, far from it. I recently purchased a nail-gun; does that mean I got rid of my hammer? No, because there are still situations where a hammer is the best tool for driving nails. I did purchase a new hammer that does a better job of driving nails than my old hammer. I now have two tools for driving nails: a nail-gun (a new tool) and a hammer (an improved version of a current tool). Think of creating a political strategy toolbox, where you are always adding new tools and improving your current tools.

Use the PDMRI cycle to improve current processes, but also think of new approaches or techniques. Don't just be creative, be crazy; go down a path you've never considered; step back from old ideas and look at them sideways. In the business world, most innovation comes not from the big corporations, but from thousands of smaller companies. Never think that because you are a small time volunteer or political neophyte that your ideas aren't worth considering—they are. Innovation in politics comes from the grass-roots, not from the top.

6. Don't allow yourself be manipulated.

Our definition of manipulation: (1) When a politician attempts to gain your support for any reason other than being productive; (2) when someone attempts to cause you to act in a manner that does not help achieve conservative goals.

The ways politicians manipulate voters are countless, we can only start to list them here:

- **Faux productivity**—politicians use various ways to make it seem like they are being productive. Letter writing, co-signing bills, preaching to the choir are just three of the examples noted earlier. The bottom line is that any action that can't be tied back to a specific goal (one that we set for the politician) is faux productivity.

- **Vote "against" the Democrat**—this is a common manipulation technique used by Republican politicians to obtain conservative votes. They portray the Democrat as being so awfully liberal that conservatives must vote against him. This allows the Republican politician to move to the center to pick up moderate

The Conservative Hand

• • • • •

voters. When you give your vote to a Republican because you are voting "against the Democrat" the Republican politician has no motivation to remain on the right. Rather, his motivation is to move left. This is raw manipulation, and its use has caused the Republican Party to shift to the left.

- **False promises**—a candidate that makes a promise they have no intention of keeping is simply trying to manipulate you. This is why we are going to demand politicians agree to our goals—and measure them on their productivity achieving those goals.

- **Misrepresenting facts**—in the 2010 Massachusetts senate election, Democrats ran ads accusing the Republican candidate of "Voting to deny emergency room care to rape victims." The reality was the Republican candidate had voted for a bill that said you couldn't force a medical worker with a religious objection to abortion to be involved in one.

These examples, along with many other forms of political manipulation, are considered par for the course for politicians. Political pundits and reporters sort of giggle under their breath and say "Nobody actually expects politicians to keep their promises or tell the truth." Maybe I'm naive to expect more out of our elected leaders, but I do.

Politicians have long viewed voters as marionettes. If they pull the right strings, they can make us move however they want.

We have to stop it; the beginning of the end is to recognize political manipulation when it occurs, call people on it, and no longer allow it to control us. Accepting political manipulation as part of the political process is not acceptable. Cut your strings.

7. All players act in their self-interest.

What is someone's self-interest? The obvious answer is money or power, but humans are more complicated than that. Take someone in Indiana raising money for earthquake relief—a purely altruistic endeavor. If something else comes up that threatens to divert funds away from their goal (say a person raising funds for flood relief), what will they do? They will fight to get the funds for earthquake relief, because they have taken on one goal as their own and not the other. Earthquake relief can be defined as this person's self-interest.

Earthquake relief vs. flood relief is an extreme example, but it makes the point: people will always prioritize their own goals ahead of the goals of others (even if both goals are deserving of support). People take up a political goal for any number of reasons. From our standpoint, it doesn't matter why they adopt it. What's important to us is that once they adopt a goal it becomes their political self-interest. A person's or group's self-interest is an issue they support.

Don't let people pry you away from pursing your self-interest by laying a guilt trip on you. Conservatives support altruistic causes; the difference is we insist the solutions actually work.

This is very different from the left's "good intentions" based solutions that often end up making matters worse (such as the *Community Reinvestment Act*—created to help low-income families buy homes, it ended up being a prime cause of the mortgage market collapse in 2008). Good intentions that make things worse are not good; they are bad intentions masquerading as good. Making things better is good.

Just as Adam Smith's invisible hand involves multiple groups pursing their self-interest producing a greater good. Our conservative invisible hand will also produce a greater good, but only if we are strict about pursing our political self-interest.

8. Define all players from our perspective.

How do we interact with a person or group? To answer that we have to know who they are (not who they claim to be), but who they are from our perspective. Are they part of the political system we're creating or outside of it? Are they supporting our process or undermining it?

Businesses define everyone by how they fit into their system. Are they a competitor, customer, employee, or supplier? We need to define everyone from our perspective so we can determine how they fit into our political system. We can then determine how we're going to interact with them. The first question you should ask when meeting someone or becoming aware of a new group is: who are they from our perspective?

- Conservatives: those with a goal of enacting conservative legislation.

- The Republican Party: a tool to achieve conservative goals.

- Republican politicians: a tool to achieve conservative goals.

- Liberals: those with a goal of enacting liberal legislation.

- Moderates (aka swing voters): easily manipulated voters without a well informed or grounded philosophical base upon which to make political decisions.

- Democratic politicians: an impediment to achieving our goals.

- The Democratic Party: an impediment to achieving our goals.

- Third-parties: an impediment to achieving our goals.

9. Form second-parties.

Organizations multiply the influence of individuals, but only if they form the right kind of organization. Big, generic organizations haven't proven to be effective in politics (at least for conservatives), they just tend to suck up resources and get in the way. Second-parties are formed to achieve specific goals, and because of their size they should be quicker on their feet.

Second-parties give us an organizational tool that really doesn't exist on the right: a political group with specific expectations. Take education as an example. The teacher's unions on the left are dedicated to maintaining a government monopoly on education. To them it's a do-or-die issue; any privatization or parental choice (such as school vouchers) must be opposed. They give Democratic politicians little choice, either do it (eliminate vouchers) or die politically. Consequently, when Barack Obama took office, one of the first things he and the Democratic congress did was eliminate the school voucher program in Washington DC. What was the Republican response? A few speeches, but for the most part it was pretty tepid. There isn't an organization on the right pushing for vouchers and school choice that matches the intensity of the teacher's unions on the left. A second-party focused on improving education using free market principles (parental choice and competition) could change that.

The second-party is the tool to drive the Republican Party to the right and achieve our goals. It is designed to apply a type of pressure to politicians that they cannot ignore so we can achieve specific conservative goals.

10. The Republican Party is the only major political party we can use as a tool to achieve our goals.

There are two primary political parties: the Democratic Party and the Republican Party. That isn't going to change anytime soon. The Democratic Party is too deeply entrenched in liberal philosophy to be moved enough to the right to achieve our goals. That leaves the Republican Party as our only practical tool, and tool is the operative word. I know a lot of people are mad at the Republican Party, I am too. Keep in mind though, it isn't the party that has failed us, it is the people who make up the party (the politicians, officials, bureaucrats, and party hacks) that have failed. Second-parties give us a lever to control those people and the party.

That doesn't mean blind loyalty to the Republican Party. We'll work *through* the Republican Party, but not *for* the Republican Party. Our goal is to enact conservative legislation, not to indulge the Republican Party.

11. Beware the political Stockholm syndrome.

The Stockholm syndrome: when hostages identify with their captors to the point that they take on the self-interest of their captors as their own.

Politics has its own version of the Stockholm syndrome: when people start to identify with a political party or politician to the point that they take on the party's or politician's self-interest as their own. Many solid conservatives joined the Republican Party during the Reagan era. Today, far too many of them are solid Republicans first, and conservatives second; putting the self-interest of the Republican Party ahead of conservative values. They fell to the political Stockholm syndrome.

We've all heard people say they are supporting a politician because "He's our guy" or "He's one of us" even though the politician's actions are at odds with what they support. This is another form of the political Stockholm syndrome. They identify so strongly with the politician that they lose the ability to judge the politician's actions. Taken to the extreme it results in a cult of personality around a politician.

Never identify with the Republican Party to the point that you start seeing its goal (electing Republicans) as more important than our goal of enacting conservative legislation. Always remember the Republican Party is a tool you are using to achieve your goals, not the other way around. The same can be said of any second-party of which you are a member. Your loyalty belongs to the second-party's *goals*, not the second-party.

Never put a politician ahead of our goals. They may have tremendous charisma and communication skills, but history has shown when you look under the hood of any politician and you'll find they really aren't that special. The hard fact is that in any community you can find a myriad of people who could do just as well (if not better) than the current holder of any political office.

12. Never engage in an activity that drives the Republican Party to the left.

People are moved by incentives. You get more of the actions you reward, and less of the actions you punish. A number of activities conservatives have engaged in are designed to move the Republican Party to the right actually have the opposite effect. Why? We've forgotten the law of unintended consequences. You get results you don't expect when you only look at an activity from one side. We need to step back from our plans and put ourselves in someone else's shoes to determine if our incentive will affect them as we expect, or if there will be an unintended consequence we hadn't accounted for. Here is a short list of some of the activities that have backfired on us and pushed the Republican Party to the left.

- **Third-parties**—as far as establishment Republicans are concerned people who support third-parties are lost voters, too difficult and expensive to regain. Their response is to shift left and look for moderate and swing voters.

- **Supporting a Democrat**—establishment Republicans believe anyone that would even consider voting for a Democrat is (by definition) a moderate, and the way to attract moderate voters is to shift to the left. It doesn't

matter how conservative the Democrat you are
supporting is, it pushes the Republican Party to the
left.

• **Punishing the Republican by voting Democratic** — see
"Never support a Democratic" above. The message
you are sending isn't "I'm punishing the Republican" it
is "I am a swing voter." The way Republicans go after
swing-voters is to shift to the left.

• **Voting "against" the Democrat** — this is a common
plea from Republicans. The Democrat is so bad that
you must hold your nose and vote for the Republican.
What this allows the Republican to do is gain
conservative support without doing anything to earn
it. Since they can use this to lock down conservative
support, it allows them to move left to look for more
support from moderates.

• **Not voting (sitting on your hands)** — this is yet another
popular tactic among conservative voters upset with a
Republican candidate. "If they won't do what we want,
we'll just stay home election day and show them."
Unfortunately, Republican candidates interpret this to
mean you are a voter that can't be counted on. Will you
show up next election or not? He doesn't know the
answer to that question. If Republican politicians don't

believe conservative voters can be counted on, they figure they have to look elsewhere for votes. That elsewhere is always to the left.

It's vital that as part of our planning stage we step back and view the plan from the angle of the person or group we are trying to affect. Will they interpret it differently? Will they find some unintended incentive in the plan to act differently than we had hoped they would? These are questions we have to know the answer to if we are going to avoid taking actions that move Republicans to the left.

13. A non-productive Republican = a Democrat.

What do Democrats do? They impede conservative goals and enact liberal legislation. What do non-productive Republicans do? They impede conservative goals and (since they aren't enacting conservative legislation) any legislation they enact must by definition be liberal legislation.

Notice I said non-productive politicians. I didn't say RINO, Rockefeller Republican, liberal Republican, or imperfect Republican. All of those can be used as tools to achieve conservative goals; they can be part of our process. And because we are constantly improving our processes, we can improve these imperfect Republicans over time by moving them to the right.

A politician that won't or can't achieve our goals though is no use to us at all. They aren't part of our process, and in fact they get in the way of our processes. From our standpoint a non-productive Republican and a Democrat is the same thing.

14. We set the goals for politicians.

Who are our leaders? Politicians would say they are, even referring to themselves as elected leaders. There is an older definition we should go with: public servant. In our American system power flows up from the citizens, not down from politicians. Politicians are supposed to follow the agenda set by the people, not the other way around. Sadly, this hasn't always been the case.

When we allow politicians to make vague promises based upon their ideas, we are allowing them to set the agenda. We want politicians to follow our agenda. That means we have to set the goals, and demand politicians achieve them. To do otherwise makes politicians our leaders. Where they would lead us only they know.

15. Use SMART goals.

S Specific. Not "I support lower taxes", but "I will cut income taxes 10% by June of this year."

M Measurable. You need some way to define if the action was completed, and it should be in the form of a yes or no question. "Were income taxes cut 10% by June of this year?" If you can't phrase the goal as a yes or no question then you should restate the goal.

A Action Oriented. *"I support* lower taxes" requires no action on the part of the politician. *"I will* cut income taxes by 10% by June of this year" does require action (the phrase "I support..." is a common hiding place for politicians as it allows them to garner votes without committing to anything; Democrats routinely say "I support our troops," but how often does that translate into action on their part?)

R Realistic. Politicians make unrealistic promises, because they know they will never be held to them. "I will cut income taxes *50%* by June of this year" is not a realistic promise.

T Time bound. Establishing a deadline allows us to hold politicians' feet to the fire for not achieving conservative goals (and properly reward them for achieving conservative goals). "I will cut income taxes 10% *by June of this year."*

16. Beware of goal creep.

As you put your plan into action, it's tempting to add little things here and there, because they are convenient to do or just seem to fit in with what you are doing at the time. Don't do it! What you end up doing is diluting your original goal, your plan, and your focus.

If something is worth doing, it is worth establishing as a separate goal and creating a separate plan for achieving it, even if it seems small and simple at the time. Poorly planned small and simple tasks have a habit of ballooning into big complicated tasks. Staying focused on your original goal and plan is the most efficient way to get things done.

17. Only measure politicians against our goals.

When you measure a politician against something that isn't one of our specific goals for them, you have essentially added another goal. It's a form of goal creep that dilutes the politician's focus. Plus, it allows someone else to set our goals (as someone had to come up with that additional goal from somewhere).

Worse, what happens when you give a politician a negative measurement against something that wasn't one of the original goals? They'll throw their hands up in the air and say "There's no pleasing those people, I accomplished their goals and they still rated me non-productive because I didn't accomplish something that wasn't a goal in the first place." That creates a huge incentive for the politician to simply ignore us.

Set the goals for politicians, and stay with them. Don't add to them, and don't subtract from them.

18. The only measurements are productive and non-productive.

We're using a binary pass/fail system. This isn't because we want to be rigid, but because it has advantages over other systems. Composite ratings and scoring systems give politicians too much wiggle room; they can achieve a conservative composite rating while supporting some pretty liberal causes. Historically they haven't moved politicians to the right. Bottom line—they don't work.

A simple productive/non-productive standard provides clarity for everyone. Politicians know exactly what is expected of them, and we know exactly what we expect out of a politician. Adding more ratings just muddies the water for everyone; what does semi-productive mean? It's a subjective standard that nobody can measure. An objective pass/fail measurement keeps everyone on the same page.

An objective measurement system forces us to create realistic goals and break larger goals down into goal-sets. We can't demand a politician achieve a goal if we think it's unrealistic. A pass/fail measurement will also cause politicians to push back if they feel the goal is unrealistic. This is a good thing. It means we will be negotiating goals with politicians and at the end of the process everyone involved will be on board with achieving the goal.

A politician is either productive or non-productive. If you don't feel the politician's activities can be described by either measurement, then consider that the goal was set incorrectly (unfocused, unrealistic, or ill-defined). You should change the goal, not the measurement.

19. The only reason to support a politician is productivity.

If you support a politician for reasons other than productivity, then you eliminate their incentive to achieve our goals. You have broken the system and made our goals secondary to someone else's goals. Charisma, experience, speaking ability, education, intelligence, or good looks are all fine qualities for a politician to have, but by themselves they don't achieve our goals.

20. Dominate the primaries.

The earlier we are involved in the election process, the more effective we will be. Establish a support campaign for your productive candidate before the primary season even starts. Also create rejection campaigns to defeat unproductive candidates. Remember, we not only work to elect candidates, we relentlessly work to defeat unproductive Republicans; the best and easiest place to do that is in the primary.

We must eliminate open primaries. Open primaries dilute our influence by allowing anybody, including Democrats to vote in a Republican primary. How can someone be the candidate for the Republican Party if non-party members help choose him?

The other important reason to close primaries is to eliminate the influence of swing-voters: people who don't belong to a political party, but insist on voting in the primaries. Swing-voters tend to be shallow thinkers that don't understand the philosophical underpinnings of various political ideas (if they did, they wouldn't swing back and forth between incompatible political positions). Consequently, they often cast their votes not because of thoughtful political reasons, but because of inconsequential concerns like who had the best television commercials or who looked better in a debate.

The primary is the ballgame for conservatives. If we can't get a productive politician nominated in the primary, we won't have the opportunity to elect one in the general election.

21. Always reward productive politicians.

We're asking politicians to bet their careers on us. As a result, we have to keep up our part of the bargain. That means always rewarding politicians for being productive—always. It also means being loyal to productive politicians. Once you have established a political relationship with a productive politician, don't abandon that politician to switch to another productive politician.

We're creating an incentive program for politicians. We'll get more of the actions we reward and less of the actions we fail to reward. If we're not loyal to productive politicians or don't consistently reward them, they won't be loyal to us or be productive. On the other hand, if we're loyal to productive politicians and consistently reward them, they'll be loyal to us and be consistently productive.

22. Be reliable.

A reliable incentive is worth more than an unreliable one. Being reliable establishes in politician's minds the level of support they can expect from us. How many people will consistently show up and vote? Will we provide support in the primary? What kind of support will we provide? Politicians need to know the answers to these questions if they are going to bet their careers on us.

We also need to establish a "negative" reliability. Remember, we're going to reject non-productive politicians. That means actively opposing and working to unseat non-productive politicians. Productive politicians need to clearly comprehend the level of opposition they'll face from us should they become non-productive politicians.

We'll create a stronger incentive for politicians to be productive by being reliable. The more reliable we become the more valuable we become. Reliable support is the biggest incentive we bring to the table.

23. Never endorse multiple Republican politicians.

Endorsing multiple candidates only dilutes our influence. Even if there are multiple productive candidates in an election, we must unite behind a single candidate. This will make us more valuable to candidates seeking our support, giving us more leverage and creating a greater incentive for politicians to achieve our goals.

Endorsing multiple candidates (and splitting our vote) has historically resulted in the election of liberal Republicans. The nomination of McCain in 2008 can largely be attributed to conservatives splitting their support early in the primary season among multiple conservative candidates.

This is an area where second-parties should work together. Independent businesses compete with each other, but that doesn't prevent them from forming associations when needed. If multiple second-parties support different candidates, it is still splitting our vote. The question to ask is: can two second-parties coordinate their activities while still being true to their goals? If so, then it would be beneficial to do it. If not, then they should avoid it. Never compromise your goal.

24. Create political holes.

This is a technique we're going to use to punish non-productive politicians, while at the same time making them aware of the support they could have obtained if they had been productive. This is the stick part of our carrot and stick, but it is vital we leave the carrot dangling in front of them also as a positive incentive to change their ways and become productive.

- **Voter holes:** If there isn't a productive politician in a race, create a voter hole by writing in a prearranged candidate name representing your second-party. This lets everyone know how many votes could have been secured in an election by a productive candidate.

- **Support holes:** A support hole is when you withdraw all support of any kind (money, signs, phone calls, anything) that will assist a candidate. This is hard for a candidate to measure, but it is intensely felt.

- **Party holes:** If you are working within the Republican Party, create holes here too. Establishment Republicans expect volunteers to work for any Republican candidate—don't. Tell them you'll be happy to provide support for specific productive Republican candidates, but flat-out refuse to do any work that might benefit a non-productive candidate. They'll get mad at you, but stick to your principles and tell them where to stick their anger. If you volunteer or work in a hospital the law says you don't have to assist in an abortion if you have a religious objection—that's just fair. If you volunteer or work in the Republican Party, nobody should be able to force you to provide support for a non-productive politician—that's just fair.

25. Reject all non-productive politicians.

Issue a rejection notice to all non-productive politicians, even if it means rejecting everyone running in the primary. Failing to reject a non-productive politician is a form of reward; you always get more of the activities you reward.

Rejection notices are more than just withdrawing support from a candidate. It involves actively working against a non-productive candidate.

By default you reject all non-Republicans (including Democrats and third-party candidates). Don't give the impression you are rejecting a non-productive Republican, but are somehow OK with a third-party candidate or Democrat by failing to reject them as well.

26. All politicians are dispensable.

Far too many non-productive politicians have stayed in office simply by positioning themselves as indispensable. Claiming their experience, knowledge, seniority, or even committee assignments make them valuable—but valuable to whom? As a rule, the longer a politician has held office the less responsive he is to his constituents and more responsive he is to...someone who isn't his constituent! The most important attributes a politician requires are humility, honesty, and common-sense. Those attributes are acquired long before taking office.

Charles de Gaulle said "The graveyards are full of indispensable men," meaning great men have come and gone throughout history, but the world always manages to carry on fine without them. There are no indispensable politicians; we'll manage to carry on fine without them.

27. Live in the real world.

Many conservative goals are large, core ideological ideas that will take years (if not decades) to achieve. Insisting they be achieved overnight is not realistic. It may provide you with a sense of personal moral victory because you "held the line," but so what? A moral victory is still a loss. This isn't a call to compromise; it is a call to stop failing and start achieving.

Nitpicking a solution to death is when you find a solution that is pretty good, but not perfect. You over focus on one part of the solution that isn't perfect and say "I can't live with this imperfection, so I'm going to oppose the entire solution." Consequently, you end up not implementing any solution and allow the status quo to stand.

People that want to maintain the status quo often use this type of argument to torpedo a solution they oppose. Don't allow yourself to be manipulated in that way. Recognize when someone is nitpicking a solution to death in an attempt to get you to oppose what is generally a good solution.

Remember, we've got a system (the PDMRI cycle) we use to improve processes. This applies to any solution we formulate. Don't look for perfect solutions. Find the best solution you can, implement it, then start running it through the PDMRI cycle to improve it. You won't achieve perfection (nothing is ever perfect), but by using a cycle focused on constant improvement you will eventually get pretty darned close. You are better off starting somewhere and then moving forward than never getting started.

Establish a goal-set; a series of smaller, achievable goals that build upon each other to eventually achieve your larger goal. There is no goal so large that it can't be achieved, but only if you break it down into a series of smaller goals. Work the smaller goals, and the larger goals will achieve themselves.

28. It's a political free market system.

Think of second-parties as operating in a political free market system. Businesses compete against each other for customers; second-parties will also compete against each other for members (the "customers" of second-parties). Poorly run second-parties, like poorly run businesses, will lose "customers" and go under. Conversely, well run second-parties, like well run businesses, will attract "customers" and grow.

Second-parties that refuse to work in conjunction with other second-parties will lose members. While second-parties are built around a single goal, their members are not single-issue voters. Members are encouraged to join and support multiple second-parties. If one second-party isn't cooperating with another second-party they also support, they'll drop the uncooperative second-party and join one with the same goal that does cooperate effectively. Also, if a member realizes his party is cooperating with a fringe, left leaning, or poorly run second-party the member will drop it in favor of another. How (and with whom) a second-party associates will have an impact on its viability.

This free market approach will act as a natural filter that eliminates incompetent second-parties—groups with a poorly focused or fringe goal; that have unmeasurable or unrealistic goal-sets; that are not transparent about their goals, leadership, or finances; who are not responsive to their membership; or who are not achieving their goal. This will leave the best, most efficient, second-parties to achieve our goals. Don't do anything to suppress this political free market process for second-parties.

Summary

What are we?

We've accepted a fundamental fact of life: everyone works in their self-interest. That means everyone works for their own goals harder than they do for the goals of others. Consequently, we have become goal oriented and established that the purpose of our involvement in politics is to accomplish specific goals. We learned to define everyone from our perspective. This allows us to understand their goals, understand how their goals affect our activities, and understand how to interact with them.

We're using those insights to create a new system. One like the free market's invisible hand that has no single leader, isn't organized from the top down, that from the outside looks like chaos, and that when allowed to operate without interference accomplishes a greater common goal. This system is our political invisible hand—the conservative hand.

The Conservative Hand

•   • • • •

We know to be proactive and set the goals for politicians, instead of allowing them to make empty promises to us. We've set a new standard for politicians: productivity, as well as a new measurement: productive vs. non-productive. No more numeric ratings and no more fuzzy standards, we're using a standard that clearly defines if a politician is achieving our goals.

We have made a commitment to stop doing the things that haven't worked in the past. This doesn't mean we'll dart from strategy to strategy in some vain hope of finding perfection. We've established a process improvement cycle. We're keeping strategies that work, even if imperfectly, and running them through the cycle to improve them, as well as creating and adopting new strategies into our toolbox.

Our new organization is the second-party. Not a primary party like the Republican Party, not a third-party, but somewhere in between. A party that will function like no political party has in the past.

We have a new plan of action which involves not just endorsing politicians, but rejecting politicians as well.

Finally, we've created a new set of rules to clarify our ideas.

What's the next step?

- Determine the goal your second-party will be built around.

- Form a second-party.

- Create your statement-of-purpose.

- Break your primary goal down into a goal-set.

- Find Republican politicians that will agree to support your goals. Support them, but only one in each race— don't split your vote between Republican politicians in any race.

- Reject all other politicians.

- Measure the politicians you support on their productivity. Continue to support the productive ones, reject the non-productive ones.

- Continually improve your processes using the PDMRI cycle. Always ask yourself: are we at a point we can review and improve our processes? If the answer is yes, then do it.

- Drop strategies that don't work, improve working strategies, and add new strategies.

Where are we heading?

Ten years from now I expect this system to look very different from what is described in this book. Twenty years from now I expect it to look different than it will ten years from now. Why? Two reasons: (1) we'll be using a quality improvement cycle (PDMRI) to continually improve our processes, and (2) because, like small businesses, second-parties will innovate in ways no one can foresee at this point.

We have created a system that fosters creativity and change. Not the left's definition of change— totally replace a working system with a new system based on theories developed in a vacuum, crossing your fingers, and declaring it a success whether it works or not (one step forward, two steps back is one thing; one giant leap forward, two giant leaps back is a risk too high to tolerate). Our definition of change is continually *improving* systems: get rid of the bad, make the good better, and add the new.

We've got a starting point. We'll get where we're going by improving our processes in incremental steps. The system we develop will be tremendously effective. Not because I designed it, but because thousands of people will improve on the original design in ways I could never anticipate, and take it to heights I could never envision.

Lagniappe

There are a few extra items I wanted to talk about that didn't fit into the flow of the book, so I've added a little lagniappe to wrap things up.

Alinsky's Rules

Saul Alinsky's *Rules for Radicals* has been in the spotlight since Barack Obama became president. It is well known that President Obama immersed himself in Alinsky's ideas; using and teaching Alinsky's techniques as a community organizer. Alinsky's book and ideas have also been adopted by progressives as a blueprint for their political strategy. I've heard any number of people suggest we should adopt Alinsky's tactics so we can fight fire with fire. I believe there are solid reasons why we should not go down that path.

Saul Alinsky has a reputation as an evil genius. When I read the book the evil part was easy to find, but the genius part was another matter. Instead of a sophisticated plan that left me awestruck, I found a juvenile mish-mash of ideas. This isn't Sun Tzu's *Art of War*, this isn't Machiavelli's *The Prince*, this isn't chess, heck I'm not even sure it's checkers. I can understand how its original target audience (college students —an immature group by definition) could take it seriously, but it's unnerving to realize there are mature adults (including some of our most important political leaders) that actually take this seriously.

There are three core ideas contained in the book: deception, manipulation, and intimidation.

Deceiving people isn't a long-term strategy for success. Trust is like a china plate. When you break it (no matter how skillfully it is repaired) you can always see where it was broken. Governments that use deception to control their citizens go to great lengths to hide the truth from them, but the truth always gets out. When people realize you have deceived them they will never fully trust you again.

The manipulation techniques taught all have one fundamental flaw: they expect you to play along. It's as though they are putting on a stage play—a bit of political theater—and everyone is an actor in the play. If everyone doesn't play their assigned part the play is a flop. Someone accused of violating a political-correctness speech code is supposed to react with shame and contrition (their part in the play), not point out that the speech code itself is absurd. Countering these techniques is simple: refuse to play your assigned part, step back, and point out the reality: "Those aren't protestors, they are people you promised $50.00 and lunch to hold printed signs and act angry. I'm not going to play the part of someone being protested, because that is not what is happening."

Alinsky's intimidation techniques really amount to making threats. He even states that threats don't have to have anything behind them, but if you make the threat loud and long enough it becomes reality in people's minds (but only in people's minds). Like the schoolyard bully, when confronted by someone who refuses to back down their "power" evaporates.

Beyond the initial point that Alinsky's ideas crumble when exposed to the light of day, there is a more fundamental reason we should avoid them. Not just dark and cynical, quite bluntly they are evil. Given Alinsky's belief that the end (always) justifies the means, what would you expect? To Alinsky nothing is off-limits—absolutely nothing. He spends a great amount of time explaining that moral questions are not only meaningless, but should be ignored. The only questions Alinsky says matters are: (1) if it will work, and (2) is it worth the cost (the cost to you, not to the people you are hurting; hurting others is not only accepted by Alinsky, it is encouraged if that's what it takes to get what you want).

Violence—Alinsky not only recommends violence, but cynically speaks as though everybody would use violence if they could. He even uses Gandhi as an example of someone who really, really, really wanted to use violence, but only held back because the circumstances didn't make it a viable option. Did Gandhi (the father of non-violent resistance) deep in his heart yearn to use violence to kill, maim, burn, and destroy? Alinsky says yes. Is it surprising that President Obama, so deeply immersed in Alinsky's philosophy, can't bring himself to condemn terrorist (or even use the word terrorism for that matter). As far as Alinsky is concerned terrorism is a perfectly valid political method.

Polarity—Alinsky doesn't use the specific term, but he describes (and praises) its use extensively: demonize a person or group, create division, and organize the rest of society against the demonized person or group. Anyone that knows even a little history understands the use of this technique in 1930's Germany directly led to the death of millions of Jews. Alinsky isn't a case of "those that forget history are doomed to repeat it." He knows the history, he just doesn't care. He takes an entire chapter to make the point that the ends always justify the means, or as he puts it: "Does this *particular* means justify this *particular* end?" Alinsky's answer to that question is always—yes it does. If you demonize a group of people to the point that it results in genocide to get your way, according to Alinsky's rules that would simply be just another "*particular* means to a *particular* end."

Ideas like deception, manipulation, intimidation, violence, and a cynical "the ends always justify the means" attitude are not part of the American design. This country was founded on a higher standard, and Americans deserve better. Progressives have no choice but to use the underhanded tactics found in Alinsky's books to hide the truth about what they are really trying to do, because when brought into the daylight their true goals and philosophy (just like a vampire) crumble into ash.

Our philosophy is based upon ideas contained in *The Declaration of Independence* and *The United States Constitution* — ideas that have stood the test of time. When you expose conservative philosophy and ideas to the daylight they don't crumble, they shine.

Election Integrity

The integrity of our election process has been declining for decades, and people (at least those in power) don't seem to care. Election fraud—dead people voting, fraudulent registrations, ballot box stuffing, counterfeit write-in ballots, corrupted voter rolls, and boxes of ballots turning up in the trunk of someone's car—has become all too acceptable. Media pundits and politicians make jokes about "voting early and often." No, make jokes is not the right phrase. They laugh about it, but they don't act as though it is a joke. They act as though it is the truth, and they think that truth is funny.

I don't think it's funny. Our freedoms, including our election rights, were purchased with the blood of countless men. No doubt many took some comfort in their last moments knowing they had sacrificed their lives to preserve our American freedoms—including our free elections. I doubt any thought "I'm spilling my life out on this battlefield so some guy can stuff a ballot box in Chicago."

Voter fraud should be right up there with child abuse as an act that is universally abhorred. An act so despised that even making jokes about it is condemned. Those that sacrificed everything to give us the gift of free elections placed a clear obligation upon us. It's time we honor that obligation and return the integrity to our election system.

One Goal Per Second Party

It has been emphasized several times in this book that a second-party should be built around achieving a single goal. Despite those warnings, it is inevitable that someone will come along and declare "We can handle multiple goals; we can do just a little bit more." Consider the following list.

- **Mission creep**: the tendency of military operations to expand the scope of their mission.

- **Feature creep**: the tendency of product designers to expand the feature set of a product.

- **Software bloat**: the continual adding of features to software that results in the software being oversized, over complicated, and slow.

- **Instruction creep**: when documentation or guidelines are expanded to the point they become too complicated or detailed to be followed.

- **Scope creep**: the adding of new tasks to already approved projects.

- **Over-engineering**: when a product is more complicated than required to fulfill its purpose.

- **Second-system effect**: tendency to take a small, efficient system and expand it into a large, bloated, inefficient monster.

All of these terms have two things in common: (1) they are all caused by trying to add "just a little bit extra" and (2) they are negative terms. Volumes have been written about how trying to do too much, taking on too many tasks, making things too complicated, or adding "just one more" thing causes serious problems. Why would anyone think this would be different with second-parties? It won't be.

Multiple goals will make your second-party fall prey to goal-creep. You will lose your focus, and inevitably one goal dominates others. Will the extra goal help you attract extra members? No, it will do just the opposite. When you try to be everything to everyone you end up being nothing to no one. Anybody suggesting a second-party take on multiple goals should be forced to sit in time-out for ten minutes (thirty minutes if they use the phrase "big tent"). One party; one goal; that's the rule. There is no "good reason" good enough to violate that rule.

A Final Note

In 1981 Auburn had lost 18 of the last 22 games against Alabama. Auburn knew its place: the *other* school in the state; they were destined to be dominated by The Crimson Tide. Auburn fans were happy if the game was close, even if they didn't win, because they had accepted their place in the world.

Pat Dye took over the Auburn football program that year. He realized there was no tangible reason for Alabama's dominance over Auburn. Both schools played in the same conference, had excellent facilities, recruited at the highest level, and had the full backing of their school's administration. The one advantage Alabama did possess was not just confidence, but swagger. Alabama acted as though dominating Auburn was their divine right, and Auburn (for some reason) had bought into it.

Prior to the 1981 game, Dye walked up to the Alabama coach and said something that would change the rivalry forever: "We're not scared of you anymore." The 'Bama coach laughed; so did the Alabama fans. After 1981 Auburn won 6 of the next 8 contests—Alabama fans stopped laughing.

In the quarter century after 1981, Auburn won 60% of the games vs. Alabama. Pat Dye changed the Auburn football program from doormat to dominant because he recognized reality when no one else did. All it took was an attitude change embodied in a simple, blunt statement: "We're not scared of you anymore."

The Conservative Hand

• • • • •

The era of Reagan is over. The country is moving to the left. Conservative stances turn off voters. We must move to the center to win elections. We must accept that we are the political minority, and just take what we can get. Over and over again we've been told—by both the media and the Republican Party—that the place of conservatism in the world has been ordained, and conservatives (for some reason) have bought into it.

Where is the tangible evidence to support this view? Polls show the majority of the country identifies themselves as conservatives (60% in some polls). Conservative books dominate every political non-fiction bestseller list. The "conservative" cable news channel has more viewers than all of the other four cable news channels combined— **COMBINED!** 1 in 5 people listening to the radio at this very moment are listening to talk radio—which is virtually 100% conservative. When Republicans run as proud conservatives (as they did in 1980, 1984, 1988, and 1994) they don't just win —they win landslides.

In 2009 neither the press nor politicians understood (or wanted to understand) the Tea Party movement. To them it was a fringe movement of citizens divorced from reality. They ignored and laughed at the Tea Party movement hoping it would go away so everything could get back to normal. It didn't go away, and nobody's laughing anymore.

The Conservative Hand

●　●●●●

Merely by standing up for ourselves we've gone from being disregarded to being a major power in modern politics—one that is striking fear in the old guard of politics. To those in the media that ridicule us; to politicians that imagine they are superior to us; to political parties that want to co-opt us; to political royal families convinced they have a divine right; to progressives striving to use political correctness to intimidate us; to those on the left that tell us the tea party is over our reply should be simple and blunt: we're not scared of you anymore.

The Origins of Our Political Ideas

The left seems to believe we oppose so many of the things they are trying to do because we don't understand their proposals or how government actually works. In a forum featuring Valerie Jarrett (one of President Obama's senior advisers) it was suggested that the Obama administration needs to create a booklet to simplify things for us in the Tea Party movement —something along the lines of a *How Government Works for Dummies* book (yes, they did say *for Dummies*). Ms. Jarrett thought that was an "excellent idea," because one of the Obama administration's biggest challenges was finding a "simple" way of communicating with us in the Tea Party movement.

In actuality, we already have a document that explains how our government works: *The United States Constitution*. The problem isn't that we don't understand what the progressive left in this country is trying to accomplish; the problem is that we clearly comprehend what the left is trying to accomplish and that their goals are not only at odds with *The United States Constitution*, but with the vision of this country laid out by the country's founders in *The Declaration of Independence* and *The Federalist Papers.*

We need to be prepared to explain not only what we believe, but why we believe it. When the left starts saying we need a *for Dummies* book, we should counter with the founding documents of the United States. We should ask them if they understand these documents; if they understand the ideas contained in them; and and if they understand how antithetical the ideas being push by today's big-government progressives are to the ideas our country was founded upon?

Our country may not be perfect, but it is still great—not because it was founded by great men, but because it was founded upon a great set of ideas. It is time we start defending the great ideas our country was founded upon. We don't need to throw anything out and start over; we don't need to transform the country; we need to hold onto what is good, and improve the things that need to be improved.

The Declaration of Independence

IN CONGRESS, July 4, 1776.

The unanimous Declaration of the thirteen united States of America,

When in the Course of human events, it becomes necessary for one people to dissolve the political bands which have connected them with another, and to assume among the powers of the earth, the separate and equal station to which the Laws of Nature and of Nature's God entitle them, a decent respect to the opinions of mankind requires that they should declare the causes which impel them to the separation.

We hold these truths to be self-evident, that all men are created equal, that they are endowed by their Creator with certain unalienable Rights, that among these are Life, Liberty and the pursuit of Happiness.—That to secure these rights, Governments are instituted among Men, deriving their just powers from the consent of the governed, —That whenever any Form of Government becomes destructive of these ends, it is the Right of the People to alter or to abolish it, and to institute new Government, laying its foundation on such principles and organizing its powers in such form, as to them shall seem most likely to effect their Safety and Happiness. Prudence, indeed, will dictate that Governments long established should not be changed for light and transient causes; and accordingly all experience hath shewn, that mankind are more disposed to suffer, while evils are sufferable, than to right themselves by abolishing the forms to which they are accustomed. But when a long train of abuses and usurpations, pursuing invariably the same Object evinces a design to reduce them under absolute Despotism, it is their right, it is their duty, to throw off such Government, and to provide new Guards for their future security.—Such has been the patient sufferance of these Colonies; and such is now the necessity which constrains them to alter their former Systems of Government. The history of the present King of Great Britain is a history of repeated injuries and usurpations, all having in direct object the establishment of an absolute Tyranny over these States. To prove this, let Facts be submitted to a candid world.

He has refused his Assent to Laws, the most wholesome and necessary for the public good.

He has forbidden his Governors to pass Laws of immediate and pressing importance, unless suspended in their operation till his Assent should be obtained; and when so suspended, he has utterly neglected to attend to them.

He has refused to pass other Laws for the accommodation of large districts of people, unless those people would relinquish the right of Representation in the Legislature, a right inestimable to them and formidable to tyrants only.

He has called together legislative bodies at places unusual, uncomfortable, and distant from the depository of their public Records, for the sole purpose of fatiguing them into compliance with his measures.

He has dissolved Representative Houses repeatedly, for opposing with manly firmness his invasions on the rights of the people.

He has refused for a long time, after such dissolutions, to cause others to be elected; whereby the Legislative powers, incapable of Annihilation, have returned to the People at large for their exercise; the State remaining in the mean time exposed to all the dangers of invasion from without, and convulsions within.

He has endeavoured to prevent the population of these States; for that purpose obstructing the Laws for Naturalization of Foreigners; refusing to pass others to encourage their migrations hither, and raising the conditions of new Appropriations of Lands.

He has obstructed the Administration of Justice, by refusing his Assent to Laws for establishing Judiciary powers.

The Conservative Hand

● ● ● ● ●

He has made Judges dependent on his Will alone, for the tenure of their offices, and the amount and payment of their salaries.

He has erected a multitude of New Offices, and sent hither swarms of Officers to harrass our people, and eat out their substance.

He has kept among us, in times of peace, Standing Armies without the Consent of our legislatures.He has affected to render the Military independent of and superior to the Civil power.

He has combined with others to subject us to a jurisdiction foreign to our constitution, and unacknowledged by our laws; giving his Assent to their Acts of pretended Legislation:

For Quartering large bodies of armed troops among us:

For protecting them, by a mock Trial, from punishment for any Murders which they should commit on the Inhabitants of these States:For cutting off our Trade with all parts of the world:

For imposing Taxes on us without our Consent: For depriving us in many cases, of the benefits of Trial by Jury:

For transporting us beyond Seas to be tried for pretended offences

For abolishing the free System of English Laws in a neighbouring Province, establishing therein an Arbitrary government, and enlarging its Boundaries so as to render it at once an example and fit instrument for introducing the same absolute rule into these Colonies:

For taking away our Charters, abolishing our most valuable Laws, and altering fundamentally the Forms of our Governments:

For suspending our own Legislatures, and declaring themselves invested with power to legislate for us in all cases whatsoever.

He has abdicated Government here, by declaring us out of his Protection and waging War against us.He has plundered our seas, ravaged our Coasts, burnt our towns, and destroyed the lives of our people.

He is at this time transporting large Armies of foreign Mercenaries to compleat the works of death, desolation and tyranny, already begun with circumstances of Cruelty & perfidy scarcely paralleled in the most barbarous ages, and totally unworthy the Head of a civilized nation.

He has constrained our fellow Citizens taken Captive on the high Seas to bear Arms against their Country, to become the executioners of their friends and Brethren, or to fall themselves by their Hands.

He has excited domestic insurrections amongst us, and has endeavoured to bring on the inhabitants of our frontiers, the merciless Indian Savages, whose known rule of warfare, is an undistinguished destruction of all ages, sexes and conditions.

In every stage of these Oppressions We have Petitioned for Redress in the most humble terms: Our repeated Petitions have been answered only by repeated injury. A Prince whose character is thus marked by every act which may define a Tyrant, is unfit to be the ruler of a free people.

Nor have We been wanting in attentions to our Brittish brethren. We have warned them from time to time of attempts by their legislature to extend an unwarrantable jurisdiction over us. We have reminded them of the circumstances of our emigration and settlement here. We have appealed to their native justice and magnanimity, and we have conjured them by the ties of our common kindred to disavow these usurpations, which, would inevitably interrupt our connections and correspondence. They too have been deaf to the voice of justice and of consanguinity. We must, therefore, acquiesce in the necessity, which denounces our Separation, and hold them, as we hold the rest of mankind, Enemies in War, in Peace Friends.

We, therefore, the Representatives of the united States of America, in General Congress, Assembled, appealing to the Supreme Judge of the world for the rectitude of our intentions, do, in the Name, and by Authority of the good People of these Colonies, solemnly publish and declare, That these United Colonies are, and of Right ought to be Free and Independent

States; that they are Absolved from all Allegiance to the British Crown, and that all political connection between them and the State of Great Britain, is and ought to be totally dissolved; and that as Free and Independent States, they have full Power to levy War, conclude Peace, contract Alliances, establish Commerce, and to do all other Acts and Things which Independent States may of right do. And for the support of this Declaration, with a firm reliance on the protection of divine Providence, we mutually pledge to each other our Lives, our Fortunes and our sacred Honor.

Button Gwinnett, Lyman Hall, George Walton, William Hooper, Joseph Hewes, John Penn, Edward Rutledge, Thomas Heyward, Jr., Thomas Lynch, Jr., Arthur Middleton, John Hancock, Samuel Chase, William Paca, Thomas Stone, Charles Carroll of Carrollton, George Wythe, Richard Henry Lee, Thomas Jefferson, Benjamin Harrison, Thomas Nelson, Jr., Francis Lightfoot Lee, Carter Braxton, Robert Morris, Benjamin Rush, Benjamin Franklin, John Morton, George Clymer, James Smith, George Taylor, James Wilson, George Ross, Caesar Rodney, George Read, Thomas McKean, William Floyd, Philip Livingston, Francis Lewis, Lewis Morris, Richard Stockton, John Witherspoon, Francis Hopkinson, John Hart, Abraham Clark, Josiah Bartlett, William Whipple, Samuel Adams, John Adams, Robert Treat Paine, Elbridge Gerry, Stephen Hopkins, William Ellery, Roger Sherman, Samuel Huntington, William Williams, Oliver Wolcott, Matthew Thornton

The Constitution of the United States

We the People of the United States, in Order to form a more perfect Union, establish Justice, insure domestic Tranquility, provide for the common defence, promote the general Welfare, and secure the Blessings of Liberty to ourselves and our Posterity, do ordain and establish this Constitution for the United States of America.

Article. I.

Section. 1.

All legislative Powers herein granted shall be vested in a Congress of the United States, which shall consist of a Senate and House of Representatives.

Section. 2.

The House of Representatives shall be composed of Members chosen every second Year by the People of the several States, and the Electors in each State shall have the Qualifications requisite for Electors of the most numerous Branch of the State Legislature.

No Person shall be a Representative who shall not have attained to the Age of twenty five Years, and been seven Years a Citizen of the United States, and who shall not, when elected, be an Inhabitant of that State in which he shall be chosen.

Representatives and direct Taxes shall be apportioned among the several States which may be included within this Union, according to their respective Numbers, which shall be determined by adding to the whole Number of free Persons, including those bound to Service for a Term of Years, and excluding Indians not taxed, three fifths of all other Persons. The actual Enumeration shall be made within three Years after the first Meeting of the Congress of the United States, and within every subsequent Term of ten Years, in such Manner as they shall by Law direct. The Number of Representatives shall not exceed one for every thirty Thousand, but each State shall have at Least one Representative; and until such enumeration shall be made, the State of New Hampshire shall be entitled to chuse three, Massachusetts eight, Rhode-Island and Providence Plantations one, Connecticut five, New-York six, New Jersey four, Pennsylvania eight, Delaware one, Maryland six, Virginia ten, North Carolina five, South Carolina five, and Georgia three.

When vacancies happen in the Representation from any State, the Executive Authority thereof shall issue Writs of Election to fill such Vacancies.

The House of Representatives shall chuse their Speaker and other Officers; and shall have the sole Power of Impeachment.

Section. 3.

The Senate of the United States shall be composed of two Senators from each State, chosen by the Legislature thereof for six Years; and each Senator shall have one Vote.

Immediately after they shall be assembled in Consequence of the first Election, they shall be divided as equally as may be into three Classes. The Seats of the Senators of the first Class shall be vacated at the Expiration of the second Year, of the second Class at the Expiration of the fourth Year, and of the third Class at the Expiration of the sixth Year, so that one third may be chosen every second Year; and if Vacancies happen by Resignation, or otherwise, during the Recess of the Legislature of any State, the Executive thereof may make temporary Appointments until the next Meeting of the Legislature, which shall then fill such Vacancies.

No Person shall be a Senator who shall not have attained to the Age of thirty Years, and been nine Years a Citizen of the United States, and who shall not, when elected, be an Inhabitant of that State for which he shall be chosen.

The Vice President of the United States shall be President of the Senate, but shall have no Vote, unless they be equally divided.

The Senate shall chuse their other Officers, and also a President pro tempore, in the Absence of the Vice President, or when he shall exercise the Office of President of the United States.

The Senate shall have the sole Power to try all Impeachments. When sitting for that Purpose, they shall be on Oath or Affirmation. When the President of the United States is tried, the Chief Justice shall preside: And no Person shall be convicted without the Concurrence of two thirds of the Members present.

Judgment in Cases of Impeachment shall not extend further than to removal from Office, and disqualification to hold and enjoy any Office of honor, Trust or Profit under the United States: but the Party convicted shall nevertheless be liable and subject to Indictment, Trial, Judgment and Punishment, according to Law.

Section. 4.

The Times, Places and Manner of holding Elections for Senators and Representatives, shall be prescribed in each State by the Legislature thereof; but the Congress may at any time by Law make or alter such Regulations, except as to the Places of chusing Senators.

The Congress shall assemble at least once in every Year, and such Meeting shall be on the first Monday in December, unless they shall by Law appoint a different Day.

Section. 5.

Each House shall be the Judge of the Elections, Returns and Qualifications of its own Members, and a Majority of each shall constitute a Quorum to do Business; but a smaller Number may adjourn from day to day, and may be authorized to compel the Attendance of absent Members, in such Manner, and under such Penalties as each House may provide.

Each House may determine the Rules of its Proceedings, punish its Members for disorderly Behaviour, and, with the Concurrence of two thirds, expel a Member.

Each House shall keep a Journal of its Proceedings, and from time to time publish the same, excepting such Parts as may in their Judgment require Secrecy; and the Yeas and Nays of the Members of either House on any question shall, at the Desire of one fifth of those Present, be entered on the Journal.

Neither House, during the Session of Congress, shall, without the Consent of the other, adjourn for more than three days, nor to any other Place than that in which the two Houses shall be sitting.

Section. 6.

The Senators and Representatives shall receive a Compensation for their Services, to be ascertained by Law, and paid out of the Treasury of the United States. They shall in all Cases, except Treason, Felony and Breach of the Peace, be privileged from Arrest during their Attendance at the Session of their respective Houses, and in going to and returning from the same; and for any Speech or Debate in either House, they shall not be questioned in any other Place.

No Senator or Representative shall, during the Time for which he was elected, be appointed to any civil Office under the Authority of the United States, which shall have been created, or the Emoluments whereof shall have been encreased during such time; and no Person holding any Office under the United States, shall be a Member of either House during his Continuance in Office.

Section. 7.

All Bills for raising Revenue shall originate in the House of Representatives; but the Senate may propose or concur with Amendments as on other Bills.

Every Bill which shall have passed the House of Representatives and the Senate, shall, before it become a Law, be presented to the President of the United States: If he approve he shall sign it, but if not he shall return it, with his Objections to that House in which it shall have originated, who shall enter the Objections at large on their Journal, and proceed to reconsider it. If after such Reconsideration two thirds of that House shall agree to pass the Bill, it shall be sent, together with the Objections, to the other House, by which it shall likewise be reconsidered, and if approved by two thirds of that House, it shall become a Law. But in all such Cases the Votes of both Houses shall be determined by yeas and Nays, and the Names of the Persons voting for and against the Bill shall be entered on the Journal of each House respectively. If any Bill shall not be returned by the President within ten Days (Sundays excepted) after it shall have been presented to him, the Same shall be a Law, in like Manner as if he had signed it, unless the Congress by their Adjournment prevent its Return, in which Case it shall not be a Law.

Every Order, Resolution, or Vote to which the Concurrence of the Senate and House of Representatives may be necessary (except on a question of Adjournment) shall be presented to the President of the United States; and before the Same shall take Effect, shall be approved by him, or being disapproved by him, shall be repassed by two thirds of the Senate and House of Representatives, according to the Rules and Limitations prescribed in the Case of a Bill.

Section. 8.

The Congress shall have Power To lay and collect Taxes, Duties, Imposts and Excises, to pay the Debts and provide for the common Defence and general Welfare of the United States; but all Duties, Imposts and Excises shall be uniform throughout the United States;

To borrow Money on the credit of the United States;

To regulate Commerce with foreign Nations, and among the several States, and with the Indian Tribes;

To establish an uniform Rule of Naturalization, and uniform Laws on the subject of Bankruptcies throughout the United States;

To coin Money, regulate the Value thereof, and of foreign Coin, and fix the Standard of Weights and Measures;

To provide for the Punishment of counterfeiting the Securities and current Coin of the United States;

To establish Post Offices and post Roads;

To promote the Progress of Science and useful Arts, by securing for limited Times to Authors and Inventors the exclusive Right to their respective Writings and Discoveries;

To constitute Tribunals inferior to the supreme Court;

To define and punish Piracies and Felonies committed on the high Seas, and Offences against the Law of Nations;

To declare War, grant Letters of Marque and Reprisal, and make Rules concerning Captures on Land and Water;

To raise and support Armies, but no Appropriation of Money to that Use shall be for a longer Term than two Years;

To provide and maintain a Navy;

To make Rules for the Government and Regulation of the land and naval Forces;

To provide for calling forth the Militia to execute the Laws of the Union, suppress Insurrections and repel Invasions;

To provide for organizing, arming, and disciplining, the Militia, and for governing such Part of them as may be employed in the Service of the United States, reserving to the States respectively, the Appointment of the Officers, and the Authority of training the Militia according to the discipline prescribed by Congress;

To exercise exclusive Legislation in all Cases whatsoever, over such District (not exceeding ten Miles square) as may, by Cession of particular States, and the Acceptance of Congress, become the Seat of the Government of the United States, and to exercise like Authority over all Places purchased by the Consent of the Legislature of the State in which the Same shall be, for the Erection of Forts, Magazines, Arsenals, dock-Yards, and other needful Buildings;—And

To make all Laws which shall be necessary and proper for carrying into Execution the foregoing Powers, and all other Powers vested by this Constitution in the Government of the United States, or in any Department or Officer thereof.

Section. 9.

The Migration or Importation of such Persons as any of the States now existing shall think proper to admit, shall not be prohibited by the Congress prior to the Year one thousand eight hundred and eight, but a Tax or duty may be imposed on such Importation, not exceeding ten dollars for each Person.

● ● ● ● ●

The Privilege of the Writ of Habeas Corpus shall not be suspended, unless when in Cases of Rebellion or Invasion the public Safety may require it.

No Bill of Attainder or ex post facto Law shall be passed.

No Capitation, or other direct, Tax shall be laid, unless in Proportion to the Census or enumeration herein before directed to be taken.

No Tax or Duty shall be laid on Articles exported from any State.

No Preference shall be given by any Regulation of Commerce or Revenue to the Ports of one State over those of another; nor shall Vessels bound to, or from, one State, be obliged to enter, clear, or pay Duties in another.

No Money shall be drawn from the Treasury, but in Consequence of Appropriations made by Law; and a regular Statement and Account of the Receipts and Expenditures of all public Money shall be published from time to time.

No Title of Nobility shall be granted by the United States: And no Person holding any Office of Profit or Trust under them, shall, without the Consent of the Congress, accept of any present, Emolument, Office, or Title, of any kind whatever, from any King, Prince, or foreign State.

● ● ● ● ●

Section. 10.

No State shall enter into any Treaty, Alliance, or Confederation; grant Letters of Marque and Reprisal; coin Money; emit Bills of Credit; make any Thing but gold and silver Coin a Tender in Payment of Debts; pass any Bill of Attainder, ex post facto Law, or Law impairing the Obligation of Contracts, or grant any Title of Nobility.

No State shall, without the Consent of the Congress, lay any Imposts or Duties on Imports or Exports, except what may be absolutely necessary for executing it's inspection Laws: and the net Produce of all Duties and Imposts, laid by any State on Imports or Exports, shall be for the Use of the Treasury of the United States; and all such Laws shall be subject to the Revision and Controul of the Congress.

No State shall, without the Consent of Congress, lay any Duty of Tonnage, keep Troops, or Ships of War in time of Peace, enter into any Agreement or Compact with another State, or with a foreign Power, or engage in War, unless actually invaded, or in such imminent Danger as will not admit of delay.

Article. II.

Section. 1.

The executive Power shall be vested in a President of the United States of America. He shall hold his Office during the Term of four Years, and, together with the Vice President, chosen for the same Term, be elected, as follows:

Each State shall appoint, in such Manner as the Legislature thereof may direct, a Number of Electors, equal to the whole Number of Senators and Representatives to which the State may be entitled in the Congress: but no Senator or Representative, or Person holding an Office of Trust or Profit under the United States, shall be appointed an Elector.

The Electors shall meet in their respective States, and vote by Ballot for two Persons, of whom one at least shall not be an Inhabitant of the same State with themselves. And they shall make a List of all the Persons voted for, and of the Number of Votes for each; which List they shall sign and certify, and transmit sealed to the Seat of the Government of the United States, directed to the President of the Senate. The President of the Senate shall, in the Presence of the Senate and House of Representatives, open all the Certificates, and the Votes shall then be counted. The Person having the greatest Number of Votes shall be the President, if such Number be a Majority of the whole Number of Electors appointed; and if there be more than one who have such Majority, and have an equal Number of Votes, then the House of Representatives shall immediately chuse by Ballot one of them for President; and if no Person have a Majority, then from the five highest on the List the said House shall in like Manner chuse the President. But in chusing the President, the Votes shall be taken by States, the Representation from each State having one Vote; A quorum for this purpose shall consist of a Member or Members from two thirds of the States, and a Majority of all the States shall be necessary to a Choice. In every Case, after the Choice of the President, the Person having the greatest Number of Votes of the Electors shall be the Vice President. But if there should remain two or more who have equal Votes, the Senate shall chuse from them by Ballot the Vice President.

The Congress may determine the Time of chusing the Electors, and the Day on which they shall give their Votes; which Day shall be the same throughout the United States.

No Person except a natural born Citizen, or a Citizen of the United States, at the time of the Adoption of this Constitution, shall be eligible to the Office of President; neither shall any Person be eligible to that Office who shall not have attained to the Age of thirty five Years, and been fourteen Years a Resident within the United States.

In Case of the Removal of the President from Office, or of his Death, Resignation, or Inability to discharge the Powers and Duties of the said Office, the Same shall devolve on the Vice President, and the Congress may by Law provide for the Case of Removal, Death, Resignation or Inability, both of the President and Vice President, declaring what Officer shall then act as President, and such Officer shall act accordingly, until the Disability be removed, or a President shall be elected.

The President shall, at stated Times, receive for his Services, a Compensation, which shall neither be increased nor diminished during the Period for which he shall have been elected, and he shall not receive within that Period any other Emolument from the United States, or any of them.

Before he enter on the Execution of his Office, he shall take the following Oath or Affirmation:—"I do solemnly swear (or affirm) that I will faithfully execute the Office of President of the United States, and will to the best of my Ability, preserve, protect and defend the Constitution of the United States."

Section. 2.

The President shall be Commander in Chief of the Army and Navy of the United States, and of the Militia of the several States, when called into the actual Service of the United States; he may require the Opinion, in writing, of the principal Officer in each of the executive Departments, upon any Subject relating to the Duties of their respective Offices, and he shall have Power to grant Reprieves and Pardons for Offences against the United States, except in Cases of Impeachment.

He shall have Power, by and with the Advice and Consent of the Senate, to make Treaties, provided two thirds of the Senators present concur; and he shall nominate, and by and with the Advice and Consent of the Senate, shall appoint Ambassadors, other public Ministers and Consuls, Judges of the supreme Court, and all other Officers of the United States, whose Appointments are not herein otherwise provided for, and which shall be established by Law: but the Congress may by Law vest the Appointment of such inferior Officers, as they think proper, in the President alone, in the Courts of Law, or in the Heads of Departments.

The President shall have Power to fill up all Vacancies that may happen during the Recess of the Senate, by granting Commissions which shall expire at the End of their next Session.

Section. 3.

He shall from time to time give to the Congress Information of the State of the Union, and recommend to their Consideration such Measures as he shall judge necessary and expedient; he may, on extraordinary Occasions, convene both Houses, or either of them, and in Case of Disagreement between them, with Respect to the Time of Adjournment, he may adjourn them to such Time as he shall think proper; he shall receive Ambassadors and other public Ministers; he shall take Care that the Laws be faithfully executed, and shall Commission all the Officers of the United States.

Section. 4.

The President, Vice President and all civil Officers of the United States, shall be removed from Office on Impeachment for, and Conviction of, Treason, Bribery, or other high Crimes and Misdemeanors.

Article III.

Section. 1.

The judicial Power of the United States shall be vested in one supreme Court, and in such inferior Courts as the Congress may from time to time ordain and establish. The Judges, both of the supreme and inferior Courts, shall hold their Offices during good Behaviour, and shall, at stated Times, receive for their Services a Compensation, which shall not be diminished during their Continuance in Office.

Section. 2.

The judicial Power shall extend to all Cases, in Law and Equity, arising under this Constitution, the Laws of the United States, and Treaties made, or which shall be made, under their Authority;—to all Cases affecting Ambassadors, other public Ministers and Consuls;—to all Cases of admiralty and maritime Jurisdiction;—to Controversies to which the United States shall be a Party;—to Controversies between two or more States;— between a State and Citizens of another State,— between Citizens of different States,—between Citizens of the same State claiming Lands under Grants of different States, and between a State, or the Citizens thereof, and foreign States, Citizens or Subjects.

In all Cases affecting Ambassadors, other public Ministers and Consuls, and those in which a State shall be Party, the supreme Court shall have original Jurisdiction. In all the other Cases before mentioned, the supreme Court shall have appellate Jurisdiction, both as to Law and Fact, with such Exceptions, and under such Regulations as the Congress shall make.

The Trial of all Crimes, except in Cases of Impeachment, shall be by Jury; and such Trial shall be held in the State where the said Crimes shall have been committed; but when not

The Conservative Hand
• • • • •

committed within any State, the Trial shall be at such Place or Places as the Congress may by Law have directed.

Section. 3.

Treason against the United States, shall consist only in levying War against them, or in adhering to their Enemies, giving them Aid and Comfort. No Person shall be convicted of Treason unless on the Testimony of two Witnesses to the same overt Act, or on Confession in open Court.

The Congress shall have Power to declare the Punishment of Treason, but no Attainder of Treason shall work Corruption of Blood, or Forfeiture except during the Life of the Person attainted.

Article. IV.

Section. 1.

Full Faith and Credit shall be given in each State to the public Acts, Records, and judicial Proceedings of every other State. And the Congress may by general Laws prescribe the Manner in which such Acts, Records and Proceedings shall be proved, and the Effect thereof.

Section. 2.

The Citizens of each State shall be entitled to all Privileges and Immunities of Citizens in the several States.

A Person charged in any State with Treason, Felony, or other Crime, who shall flee from Justice, and be found in another

• • • • •
A Manifesto to Achieve Conservative Goals
129

State, shall on Demand of the executive Authority of the State from which he fled, be delivered up, to be removed to the State having Jurisdiction of the Crime.

No Person held to Service or Labour in one State, under the Laws thereof, escaping into another, shall, in Consequence of any Law or Regulation therein, be discharged from such Service or Labour, but shall be delivered up on Claim of the Party to whom such Service or Labour may be due.

Section. 3.

New States may be admitted by the Congress into this Union; but no new State shall be formed or erected within the Jurisdiction of any other State; nor any State be formed by the Junction of two or more States, or Parts of States, without the Consent of the Legislatures of the States concerned as well as of the Congress.

The Congress shall have Power to dispose of and make all needful Rules and Regulations respecting the Territory or other Property belonging to the United States; and nothing in this Constitution shall be so construed as to Prejudice any Claims of the United States, or of any particular State.

Section. 4.

The United States shall guarantee to every State in this Union a Republican Form of Government, and shall protect each of them against Invasion; and on Application of the Legislature, or of the Executive (when the Legislature cannot be convened), against domestic Violence.

Article. V.

The Congress, whenever two thirds of both Houses shall deem it necessary, shall propose Amendments to this Constitution, or, on the Application of the Legislatures of two thirds of the several States, shall call a Convention for proposing Amendments, which, in either Case, shall be valid to all Intents and Purposes, as Part of this Constitution, when ratified by the Legislatures of three fourths of the several States, or by Conventions in three fourths thereof, as the one or the other Mode of Ratification may be proposed by the Congress; Provided that no Amendment which may be made prior to the Year One thousand eight hundred and eight shall in any Manner affect the first and fourth Clauses in the Ninth Section of the first Article; and that no State, without its Consent, shall be deprived of its equal Suffrage in the Senate.

Article. VI.

All Debts contracted and Engagements entered into, before the Adoption of this Constitution, shall be as valid against the United States under this Constitution, as under the Confederation.

This Constitution, and the Laws of the United States which shall be made in Pursuance thereof; and all Treaties made, or which shall be made, under the Authority of the United States, shall be the supreme Law of the Land; and the Judges in every State shall be bound thereby, any Thing in the Constitution or Laws of any State to the Contrary notwithstanding.

The Senators and Representatives before mentioned, and the Members of the several State Legislatures, and all executive and judicial Officers, both of the United States and of the several States, shall be bound by Oath or Affirmation, to support this Constitution; but no religious Test shall ever be required as a Qualification to any Office or public Trust under the United States.

Article. VII.

The Ratification of the Conventions of nine States, shall be sufficient for the Establishment of this Constitution between the States so ratifying the Same.

The Word, "the," being interlined between the seventh and eighth Lines of the first Page, the Word "Thirty" being partly written on an Erazure in the fifteenth Line of the first Page, The Words "is tried" being interlined between the thirty second and thirty third Lines of the first Page and the Word "the" being interlined between the forty third and forty fourth Lines of the second Page.

Attest William Jackson Secretary

Done in Convention by the Unanimous Consent of the States present the Seventeenth Day of September in the Year of our Lord one thousand seven hundred and Eighty seven and of the Independence of the United States of America the Twelfth In witness whereof We have hereunto subscribed our Names,

G°. Washington
President and deputy from Virginia

Delaware
Geo: Read
Gunning Bedford jun
John Dickinson
Richard Bassett
Jaco: Broom

Maryland
James McHenry
Dan of St Thos. Jenifer
Danl. Carroll

Virginia
John Blair
James Madison Jr.

North Carolina
Wm. Blount
Richd. Dobbs Spaight
Hu Williamson

South Carolina
J. Rutledge
Charles Cotesworth Pinckney
Charles Pinckney
Pierce Butler

Georgia
William Few
Abr Baldwin

New Hampshire
John Langdon
Nicholas Gilman

Massachusetts
Nathaniel Gorham
Rufus King

Connecticut
Wm. Saml. Johnson
Roger Sherman

New York
Alexander Hamilton

New Jersey
Wil: Livingston
David Brearley
Wm. Paterson
Jona: Dayton

Pennsylvania
B Franklin
Thomas Mifflin
Robt. Morris
Geo. Clymer
Thos. FitzSimons

The Conservative Hand

●   ● ● ● ●

Jared Ingersoll
James Wilson
Gouv Morris

The Bill of Rights

Congress of the United States,

begun and held at the City of New-York, on Wednesday the fourth of March, one thousand seven hundred and eighty nine.

THE Conventions of a number of the States, having at the time of their adopting the Constitution, expressed a desire, in order to prevent misconstruction or abuse of its powers, that further declaratory and restrictive clauses should be added: And as extending the ground of public confidence in the Government, will best ensure the beneficent ends of its institution.

RESOLVED by the Senate and House of Representatives of the United States of America, in Congress assembled, two thirds of both Houses concurring, that the following Articles be proposed to the Legislatures of the several States, as amendments to the Constitution of the United States, all, or any of which Articles, when ratified by three fourths of the said Legislatures, to be valid to all intents and purposes, as part of the said Constitution; viz.

ARTICLES in addition to, and Amendment of the Constitution of the United States of America, proposed by Congress, and ratified by the Legislatures of the several States, pursuant to the fifth Article of the original Constitution.

Amendment I

Congress shall make no law respecting an establishment of religion, or prohibiting the free exercise thereof; or abridging the freedom of speech, or of the press; or the right of the people peaceably to assemble, and to petition the Government for a redress of grievances.

Amendment II

A well regulated Militia, being necessary to the security of a free State, the right of the people to keep and bear Arms, shall not be infringed.

Amendment III

No Soldier shall, in time of peace be quartered in any house, without the consent of the Owner, nor in time of war, but in a manner to be prescribed by law.

Amendment IV

The right of the people to be secure in their persons, houses, papers, and effects, against unreasonable searches and seizures, shall not be violated, and no Warrants shall issue, but upon probable cause, supported by Oath or affirmation, and particularly describing the place to be searched, and the persons or things to be seized.

Amendment V

No person shall be held to answer for a capital, or otherwise infamous crime, unless on a presentment or indictment of a Grand Jury, except in cases arising in the land or naval forces, or in the Militia, when in actual service in time of War or public danger; nor shall any person be subject for the same offence to be twice put in jeopardy of life or limb; nor shall be compelled in any criminal case to be a witness against himself, nor be deprived of life, liberty, or property, without due process of law; nor shall private property be taken for public use, without just compensation.

Amendment VI

In all criminal prosecutions, the accused shall enjoy the right to a speedy and public trial, by an impartial jury of the State and district wherein the crime shall have been committed, which district shall have been previously ascertained by law, and to be informed of the nature and cause of the accusation;

to be confronted with the witnesses against him; to have compulsory process for obtaining witnesses in his favor, and to have the Assistance of Counsel for his defence.

Amendment VII

In Suits at common law, where the value in controversy shall exceed twenty dollars, the right of trial by jury shall be preserved, and no fact tried by a jury, shall be otherwise re-examined in any Court of the United States, than according to the rules of the common law.

Amendment VIII

Excessive bail shall not be required, nor excessive fines imposed, nor cruel and unusual punishments inflicted.

Amendment IX

The enumeration in the Constitution, of certain rights, shall not be construed to deny or disparage others retained by the people.

Amendment X

The powers not delegated to the United States by the Constitution, nor prohibited by it to the States, are reserved to the States respectively, or to the people.

Amendment XI

The Judicial power of the United States shall not be construed to extend to any suit in law or equity, commenced or prosecuted against one of the United States by Citizens of another State, or by Citizens or Subjects of any Foreign State.

Amendment XII

The Electors shall meet in their respective states and vote by ballot for President and Vice-President, one of whom, at least, shall not be an inhabitant of the same state with themselves; they shall name in their ballots the person voted for as President, and in distinct ballots the person voted for as Vice-President, and they shall make distinct lists of all persons voted for as President, and of all persons voted for as Vice-President, and of the number of votes for each, which lists they shall sign and certify, and transmit sealed to the seat of the government of the United States, directed to the President of the Senate; — the President of the Senate shall, in the presence of the Senate and House of Representatives, open all the certificates and the votes shall then be counted; — The person having the greatest number of votes for President, shall be the President, if such number be a majority of the whole number of Electors appointed; and if no person have such majority, then from the persons having the highest numbers not exceeding three on the list of those voted for as President, the House of Representatives shall choose immediately, by ballot, the President. But in choosing the President, the votes shall be taken by states, the representation from each state having one vote; a quorum for this purpose shall consist of a member or members from two-thirds of the states, and a majority of all the states shall be necessary to a choice. [And if the House of Representatives shall not choose a President whenever the right of choice shall devolve upon them, before the fourth day of March next following, then the Vice-President shall act as President, as in case of the death or other constitutional disability of the President.] The person having the greatest number of votes as Vice-President, shall be the Vice-President, if such number be a majority of the whole number of Electors appointed, and if no person have a majority, then from the two highest numbers on the list, the Senate shall choose the Vice-President; a quorum for the purpose shall consist of two-thirds of the whole number of Senators, and a majority of the whole number shall be necessary to a choice. But no person constitutionally ineligible to the office of President shall be eligible to that of Vice-President of the United States.

Amendment XIII

Section 1. Neither slavery nor involuntary servitude, except as a punishment for crime whereof the party shall have been duly convicted, shall exist within the United States, or any place subject to their jurisdiction.

Section 2. Congress shall have power to enforce this article by appropriate legislation.

Amendment XIV

Section 1. All persons born or naturalized in the United States, and subject to the jurisdiction thereof, are citizens of the United States and of the State wherein they reside. No State shall make or enforce any law which shall abridge the privileges or immunities of citizens of the United States; nor shall any State deprive any person of life, liberty, or property, without due process of law; nor deny to any person within its jurisdiction the equal protection of the laws.

Section 2. Representatives shall be apportioned among the several States according to their respective numbers, counting the whole number of persons in each State, excluding Indians not taxed. But when the right to vote at any election for the choice of electors for President and Vice-President of the United States, Representatives in Congress, the Executive and Judicial officers of a State, or the members of the Legislature thereof, is denied to any of the male inhabitants of such State, being twenty-one years of age,* and citizens of the United States, or in any way abridged, except for participation in rebellion, or other crime, the basis of representation therein shall be reduced in the proportion which the number of such male citizens shall bear to the whole number of male citizens twenty-one years of age in such State.

Section 3. No person shall be a Senator or Representative in Congress, or elector of President and Vice-President, or hold any office, civil or military, under the United States, or under any State, who, having previously taken an oath, as a member of Congress, or as an officer of the United States, or as a member of any State legislature, or as an executive or judicial officer of any State, to support the Constitution of the United States, shall have engaged in insurrection or rebellion against the same, or given aid or comfort to the enemies thereof. But Congress may by a vote of two-thirds of each House, remove such disability.

Section 4. The validity of the public debt of the United States, authorized by law, including debts incurred for payment of pensions and bounties for services in suppressing insurrection or rebellion, shall not be questioned. But neither the United States nor any State shall assume or pay any debt or obligation incurred in aid of insurrection or rebellion against the United States, or any claim for the loss or emancipation of any slave; but all such debts, obligations and claims shall be held illegal and void.

Section 5. The Congress shall have the power to enforce, by appropriate legislation, the provisions of this article.

Amendment XV

Section 1. The right of citizens of the United States to vote shall not be denied or abridged by the United States or by any State on account of race, color, or previous condition of servitude

Section 2. The Congress shall have the power to enforce this article by appropriate legislation.

Amendment XVI

The Congress shall have power to lay and collect taxes on incomes, from whatever source derived, without apportionment among the several States, and without regard to any census or enumeration.

Amendment XVII

The Senate of the United States shall be composed of two Senators from each State, elected by the people thereof, for six years; and each Senator shall have one vote. The electors in each State shall have the qualifications requisite for electors of the most numerous branch of the State legislatures.

When vacancies happen in the representation of any State in the Senate, the executive authority of such State shall issue writs of election to fill such vacancies: *Provided*, That the legislature of any State may empower the executive thereof to make temporary appointments until the people fill the vacancies by election as the legislature may direct.

This amendment shall not be so construed as to affect the election or term of any Senator chosen before it becomes valid as part of the Constitution.

Amendment XVIII

Section 1. After one year from the ratification of this article the manufacture, sale, or transportation of intoxicating liquors within, the importation thereof into, or the exportation thereof from the United States and all territory subject to the jurisdiction thereof for beverage purposes is hereby prohibited.

Section 2. The Congress and the several States shall have concurrent power to enforce this article by appropriate legislation.

Section 3. This article shall be inoperative unless it shall have been ratified as an amendment to the Constitution by the legislatures of the several States, as provided in the Constitution, within seven years from the date of the submission hereof to the States by the Congress.

Amendment XIX

The right of citizens of the United States to vote shall not be denied or abridged by the United States or by any State on account of sex.

Congress shall have power to enforce this article by appropriate legislation.

Amendment XX

Section 1. The terms of the President and the Vice President shall end at noon on the 20th day of January, and the terms of Senators and Representatives at noon on the 3d day of January, of the years in which such terms would have ended if this article had not been ratified; and the terms of their successors shall then begin.

Section 2. The Congress shall assemble at least once in every year, and such meeting shall begin at noon on the 3d day of January, unless they shall by law appoint a different day.

Section 3. If, at the time fixed for the beginning of the term of the President, the President elect shall have died, the Vice President elect shall become President. If a President shall not have been chosen before the time fixed for the beginning of his term, or if the President elect shall have failed to qualify, then the Vice President elect shall act as President until a President shall have qualified; and the Congress may by law provide for the case wherein neither a President elect nor a Vice President shall have qualified, declaring who shall then act as President, or the manner in which one who is to act shall be selected, and such person shall act accordingly until a President or Vice President shall have qualified.

Section 4. The Congress may by law provide for the case of the death of any of the persons from whom the House of Representatives may choose a President whenever the right of choice shall have devolved upon them, and for the case of the death of any of the persons from whom the Senate may choose a Vice President whenever the right of choice shall have devolved upon them.

Section 5. Sections 1 and 2 shall take effect on the 15th day of October following the ratification of this article.

Section 6. This article shall be inoperative unless it shall have been ratified as an amendment to the Constitution by the legislatures of three-fourths of the several States within seven years from the date of its submission.

Amendment XXI

Section 1. The eighteenth article of amendment to the Constitution of the United States is hereby repealed.

Section 2. The transportation or importation into any State, Territory, or Possession of the United States for delivery or use therein of intoxicating liquors, in violation of the laws thereof, is hereby prohibited.

Section 3. This article shall be inoperative unless it shall have been ratified as an amendment to the Constitution by conventions in the several States, as provided in the Constitution, within seven years from the date of the submission hereof to the States by the Congress.

Amendment XXII

Section 1. No person shall be elected to the office of the President more than twice, and no person who has held the office of President, or acted as President, for more than two years of a term to which some other person was elected President shall be elected to the office of President more than once. But this Article shall not apply to any person holding the office of President when this Article was proposed by Congress, and shall not prevent any person who may be holding the office of President, or acting as President, during the term within which this Article becomes operative from holding the office of President or acting as President during the remainder of such term.

Section 2. This article shall be inoperative unless it shall have been ratified as an amendment to the Constitution by the legislatures of three-fourths of the several States within seven years from the date of its submission to the States by the Congress.

Amendment XXIII

Section 1. The District constituting the seat of Government of the United States shall appoint in such manner as Congress may direct:

A number of electors of President and Vice President equal to the whole number of Senators and Representatives in Congress to which the District would be entitled if it were a State, but in no event more than the least populous State; they shall be in addition to those appointed by the States, but they shall be considered, for the purposes of the election of President and Vice President, to be electors appointed by a State; and they shall meet in the District and perform such duties as provided by the twelfth article of amendment.

Section 2. The Congress shall have power to enforce this article by appropriate legislation.

Amendment XXIV

Section 1. The right of citizens of the United States to vote in any primary or other election for President or Vice President, for electors for President or Vice President, or for Senator or Representative in Congress, shall not be denied or abridged by the United States or any State by reason of failure to pay poll tax or other tax.

Section 2. The Congress shall have power to enforce this article by appropriate legislation.

Amendment XXV

Section 1. In case of the removal of the President from office or of his death or resignation, the Vice President shall become President.

Section 2. Whenever there is a vacancy in the office of the Vice President, the President shall nominate a Vice President who shall take office upon confirmation by a majority vote of both Houses of Congress.

Section 3. Whenever the President transmits to the President pro tempore of the Senate and the Speaker of the House of Representatives his written declaration that he is unable to discharge the powers and duties of his office, and until he transmits to them a written declaration to the contrary, such powers and duties shall be discharged by the Vice President as Acting President.

Section 4. Whenever the Vice President and a majority of either the principal officers of the executive departments or of such other body as Congress may by law provide, transmit to the President pro tempore of the Senate and the Speaker of the House of Representatives their written declaration that the President is unable to discharge the powers and duties of his office, the Vice President shall immediately assume the powers and duties of the office as Acting President.

Thereafter, when the President transmits to the President pro tempore of the Senate and the Speaker of the House of Representatives his written declaration that no inability exists, he shall resume the powers and duties of his office unless the Vice President and a majority of either the principal officers of the executive department or of such other body as Congress may by law provide, transmit within four days to the President pro tempore of the Senate and the Speaker of the House of Representatives their written declaration that the President is unable to discharge the powers and duties of his office. Thereupon Congress shall decide the issue, assembling within forty-eight hours for that purpose if not in session. If the Congress, within twenty-one days after receipt of the latter written declaration, or, if Congress is not in session, within twenty-one days after Congress is required to assemble, determines by two-thirds vote of both Houses that the President is unable to discharge the powers and duties of his office, the Vice President shall continue to discharge the same as Acting President; otherwise, the President shall resume the powers and duties of his office.

Amendment XXVI

Section 1. The right of citizens of the United States, who are eighteen years of age or older, to vote shall not be denied or abridged by the United States or by any State on account of age.

Section 2. The Congress shall have power to enforce this article by appropriate legislation.

Amendment XXVII

No law, varying the compensation for the services of the Senators and Representatives, shall take effect, until an election of representatives shall have intervened.

Made in the USA
Lexington, KY
10 December 2012